Syllabus of Entrance Examinations

暨南大学、华侨大学
联合招生委员会办公室

暨南大学　华侨大学联合招收港澳地区、台湾省、华侨、华人及其他外籍学生

入学考试复习大纲

（2016—2020）

顾　问◎张荣华　　主　编◎庄友明

暨南大学出版社
JINAN UNIVERSITY PRESS

中国・广州

图书在版编目（CIP）数据

暨南大学、华侨大学联合招收港澳地区、台湾省、华侨、华人及其他外籍学生入学考试复习大纲.2016—2020/庄友明主编.—广州：暨南大学出版社，2015.5（2017.4 重印）
ISBN 978－7－5668－1408－1

Ⅰ.①暨…　Ⅱ.①庄…　Ⅲ.①高等学校—入学考试—考试大纲—广州市—2016—2020　Ⅳ.①G642.474

中国版本图书馆 CIP 数据核字(2015)第 097991 号

暨南大学、华侨大学联合招收港澳地区、台湾省、华侨、华人及其他外籍学生入学考试复习大纲（2016—2020）
JINAN DAXUE HUAQIAO DAXUE LIANHE ZHAOSHOU GANGAO DIQU TAIWANSHENG HUAQIAO HUAREN JI QITA WAIJI XUESHENG RUXUE KAOSHI FUXI DAGANG（2016—2020）
主　编：庄友明

出 版 人：徐义雄
责任编辑：曹　军
责任校对：黄志波
责任印制：汤慧君　周一丹

出版发行：暨南大学出版社（510630）
电　　话：总编室（8620）85221601
营销部（8620）85225284　85228291　85228292（邮购）
传　　真：（8620）85221583（办公室）　85223774（营销部）
网　　址：http://www.jnupress.com　http://press.jnu.edu.cn
排　　版：广州市天河星辰文化发展部照排中心
印　　刷：佛山市浩文彩色印刷有限公司
开　　本：787mm×1092mm　1/16
印　　张：8.5
字　　数：200 千
版　　次：2015 年 5 月第 1 版
印　　次：2017 年 4 月第 2 次
印　　数：3001—6000 册
定　　价：29.80 元

前　言

2014 年 11 月，在国务院侨务办公室的大力支持下，暨南大学、华侨大学两校联合组团，为修订《暨南大学、华侨大学联合招收港澳地区、台湾省、华侨、华人及其他外籍学生入学考试复习大纲 2016—2020》（以下简称《入学考试复习大纲（2016—2020）》），到香港、澳门进行了该主题的调研工作。在调研期间，调研小组深入港澳部分中学，与学校的领导及各个科目的教师进行了认真的座谈，广泛听取了各种意见。调研结束后，暨南大学、华侨大学联合招生委员会办公室（以下简称两校联招办）委托暨南大学华文学院预科部对考试大纲进行了研讨和修改。新的两校联招考试大纲，将更加适合港澳台及海外学生的学习和考试。

《入学考试复习大纲（2016—2020）》包括中国语文、数学、英语、历史、地理、物理、化学、生物八科考试大纲及样卷和答案。

为了更加适应港澳地区、台湾省、华侨、华人及其他外籍学生报考暨南大学、华侨大学，暨南大学、华侨大学联合对外招生入学考试一般在每年的五月上旬举行，具体考试日期见当年的“招生简章”。考试实行“3 + X”形式，即中国语文、数学、英语为必考科目，历史、地理、物理、化学、生物任选一科或多科，报考医学类必选生物，化学、物理选一。

为了有效地帮助和指导港澳地区、台湾省、华侨、华人及其他外籍学生报考暨南大学、华侨大学，暨南大学华文学院预科部还组织教师编写了与新考纲配套的各科复习丛书。

我们热诚欢迎港澳地区、台湾省、华侨、华人及其他外籍学生报考两校。

暨南大学、华侨大学联合招生委员会办公室

2015 年 3 月

目录
CONTENTS

中国语文

考试要求

中国语文科主要考查考生在中国语言、文学和文化方面的一般知识，以及阅读能力（包括阅读现代文和文言文的能力），用语言文字表达思想感情的能力。

考试范围与内容

中国语文科考试内容包括基础知识、阅读理解和语言文字表达三部分。

一、基础知识

（1）能够掌握汉字发展及汉字结构的一般知识（如字体的历史演变、汉字的结构等）；能够识别和改正错别字。

（2）能够借助词汇知识辨析多义词在具体语言环境中的意义；能够正确使用词语（包括成语、同义词和反义词）；能够辨析词语的感情色彩。

（3）能够借助语法和逻辑知识判断句子是否正确、通顺，并能够识别和改正一般的病句（病句类型主要为：语序不当、搭配不当、成分残缺或赘余、结构混乱、表意不明、不合逻辑等）。

（4）能够正确使用标点符号。

（5）掌握比喻、比拟、借代、夸张、对偶、排比、设问、反问、反语、双关、顶针等常用修辞手法的特点，并能借以分析文章中运用的修辞手法。

（6）能正确理解比较复杂的单句和简单的复句，正确使用关联词。

（7）了解古体诗、近体诗（律诗、绝句）、词、散文（哲理、抒情、叙事、写人、游记）、小说的主要特点；能运用这些文体知识分析文章、诗词的体裁。

（8）了解中外著名作家及其代表作品。对中国历代著名作家，应掌握其姓名、常用别号、别称、生活时代（朝代）、身份（诗人、词人、散文家、小说家等）；对中外名家名篇，应掌握其作者、成书时代（或写作时代）及相关的文学常识。

（9）了解中国古代文化的一般知识。

（10）能够识记常见的名句名篇。

二、阅读理解

（一）现代文阅读

（1）能够正确理解常用词语在文中的含义。

（2）能够分析文章的结构层次，把握文章思路。

（3）能够筛选文中的信息，分析概括文章的内容和作者的思想感情。

（4）能够鉴赏文学作品的形象、语言和艺术特色。

（二）文言文阅读

（1）理解常见文言实词在文中的含义（包括通假字、古今异义等）。

（2）掌握之、其、以、于、而、则、乃、与等常用虚词的主要用法。

（3）了解特殊的文言句式和用法（包括判断句、被动句、倒装句、省略句、词类活用、固定结构等）。

（4）能够阅读浅易的文言文，并能将文言文语句翻译成规范的现代汉语。

（5）能够筛选文中的信息，分析和概括文章（包括古诗词）的内容。

三、语言文字表达

（一）语言文字表达应用

能够准确扩展语句，压缩语段，仿写句子，写作常见的应用文。

（二）作文

（1）能够理解所给材料或命题的意义、范围和要求。

（2）言之有物，中心明确，思想感情健康。

（3）条理清楚，段落分明，详略得当，结构完整。

（4）用词恰当，句子合乎语法和逻辑，正确使用标点符号，不写错别字。

考试形式

中国语文科只设一份试卷，采用闭卷、书面作答的考试形式。考试时间为 150 分钟，试卷满分为 150 分。

试卷结构与题型

中国语文科试卷由三部分组成。

第一部分为基础知识，题型有单项选择题、判断题和填空题，共计 38 分。

第二部分为阅读理解，包括现代文、文言文和诗词阅读，题型有单项选择题、翻译题和简答题等，共计 42 分（文言文阅读部分，有 12 分在本大纲所附阅读篇目中拟题）。

第三部分为语言文字表达，其中的语言文字表达应用，题型有扩写题、缩写题、仿写题等，占 10 分；作文（材料作文与命题作文二选一），占 60 分。共计 70 分。

考生复习参考资料

1. 温宗军．暨南大学、华侨大学联合招收港澳地区、台湾省、华侨、华人及其他外籍学生入学考试复习丛书·中国语文．广州：暨南大学出版社，2015.

2. 温宗军，袁忠群，林娟．暨南大学、华侨大学两校联招及全国联招2004—2011年试题详解丛书·语文．广州：暨南大学出版社，2013.

3. 温宗军，张训涛．暨南大学、华侨大学及全国联招考试模拟试题丛书·语文．广州：暨南大学出版社，2013.

附：阅读篇目

第一单元　诗　词

一、《诗经》两首

　　关雎

　　蓼莪

二、国殇　　屈原

三、孔雀东南飞（并序）　　《乐府诗集》

四、《古诗十九首》两首

　　西北有高楼

　　涉江采芙蓉

五、唐诗六首

　　出塞　　王昌龄

　　山居秋暝　　王维

　　将进酒　　李白

　　兵车行　　杜甫

　　长恨歌　　白居易

　　锦瑟　　李商隐

六、词五首

　　虞美人　　李煜

　　雨霖铃　　柳永

　　念奴娇·赤壁怀古　　苏轼

　　一剪梅　　李清照

　　永遇乐·京口北固亭怀古　　辛弃疾

七、现代诗四首

　　再别康桥　　徐志摩

　　死水　　闻一多

　　雨巷　　戴望舒

　　致橡树　　舒婷

第二单元　散　文（一）

八、烛之武退秦师	《左转》
九、荆轲刺秦王	《战国策》
十、季氏将伐颛臾	《论语》
十一、齐桓晋文之事	《孟子》
十二、庖丁解牛	《庄子》
十三、劝学	《荀子》
十四、过秦论	贾谊
十五、信陵君窃符救赵	《史记》
十六、师说	韩愈
十七、捕蛇者说	柳宗元
十八、六国论	苏洵

第三单元　散　文（二）

十九、出师表	诸葛亮
二十、陈情表	李密
二十一、归去来兮辞	陶渊明
二十二、兰亭集序	王羲之
二十三、醉翁亭记	欧阳修
二十四、项脊轩志	归有光
二十五、祭妹文	袁枚
二十六、登泰山记	姚鼐

第四单元　散　文（三）

二十七、短文三篇	
热爱生命	蒙田
人是一根能思想的苇草	帕斯卡尔
信条	富尔格姆
二十八、故都的秋	郁达夫
二十九、语言的演变	吕叔湘
三十、汉字的结构	左民安
三十一、我与地坛（节选）	史铁生

第五单元　小说、戏剧

三十二、窦娥冤（节选）	关汉卿
三十三、失街亭	罗贯中

附　录

样卷

暨南大学、华侨大学联合招收港澳地区、台湾省、华侨、华人及其他外籍学生入学考试样题

科目：中国语文

答卷时间：150 分钟

一、基础知识

（本题分选择题、非选择题两大部分。选择题的答案请填涂在答题卡上“选择题区”与题号、答案相对应的方框中；非选择题的答案则请填写在答题卡“非选择题答题区”中与题号相对应的位置上。共 38 分）

【选择题】

（一）单项选择题（每题 3 分，共 30 分）

1. 下列各组词语中没有错别字的是哪一组？

A. 吉详　开宗明义　寥若星辰　生在福中不知福

B. 妥帖　心率不齐　长嘘短叹　不以一眚掩大德

C. 通辑　个中三昧　无妄之灾　无所不用其及

D. 镌刻　杯水车薪　不修边幅　树犹如此，人何以堪

2. 下列各句中加方框的关联词使用不当的是哪一项？

A. [除非]是到了春天，[否则]你就看不到这满山遍野的杜鹃花。

B. [无论]困难有多大，我们[都]能克服。

C. 陈老莲在当时是艺术圈内无人不晓的人物，[而且]受到社会的普遍喜爱，[所以]他创造了群众喜欢的娱乐工具——叶子，并用它来传播《水浒》人物画。

D. [尽管]专家学者提出了很多有创见的教育教学理论，许多知名教师也总结出不少教学模式，[但是]如果语文课还是按过去的教法，教学效率就很难提高。

3. 依次填入下列各句横线处的词语，哪一项最为恰当？

①改革开放 30 年后的今天，公务员队伍______化建设已经有了制度保障。

②现代科技的发展日新月异，______从前的幻想今天都有可能成为现实。

③到半夜，小说终于脱稿了，他______地摸着胡子，长长地松了口气。

A. 年轻　以至　踌躇满志　　B. 年青　以致　踌躇满志

C. 年轻　以致　自鸣得意　　D. 年青　以至　自鸣得意

4. 下列各句中加方框的成语，哪一个使用最为恰当？

A. 二十一世纪是中华民族实现伟大复兴的世纪，[河东狮吼]，巨龙腾飞，指日

可待。

B. 国家机关工作人员因事久假不归的，应教育说服本人返回原单位工作；说服无效，仍坚持离职的，原单位可按自动离职处理。

C. 树立科学发展观，加快社会主义新农村建设，需要干部与群众转变观念，积极参与，切不可胶柱鼓瑟，止步不前。

D. 位于市中心的金源大厦堪称本市的标志性建筑，35 层的大楼气宇轩昂，巍然屹立，被人们称为“金融中心”。

5. 下列各句中，没有语病的是哪一项？

A. 近来，对于谷歌未经合法授权擅自扫描收录使用中国作家作品的行为，引起了中国作家们的强烈不满，为此，谷歌首次公开道歉。

B. 学生如果看不到自身发展所具有的主动性和创造性，而一味盲目模仿“考场满分作文”，那么就会变成束缚写作能力发展的枷锁。

C. 北京时间 9 月 15 日，中国排协召开新闻发布会正式宣布，原中国女排助理教练俞觉敏接替王宝泉，执掌中国女排国家队主教练。

D. 针对西南丰水地区今年为何出现百年不遇的严重干旱这一问题，水利部负责人分析指出，降雨少、来水少、蓄水少是主要原因。

6. 下列各项中，标点符号使用正确的是哪一项？

A. 最近多名官员因贪污受贿被判刑，民众无不拍手称快，但人们还在关注着检察机关对那些行贿者将如何处置？

B. 层层的叶子中间，零星地点缀着些白花，有袅娜地开着的，有羞涩地打着朵儿的；正如一粒粒的明珠，又如碧天里的星星，又如刚出浴的美人。

C. “防治手足口病是关系民生的大事情，”省领导在慰问患者及其他人员时说：“必须坚持生命第一的理念，坚决打赢这场疫情阻击战。”

D. 国家有关法律文件对非法制造、贩卖、运输、持有毒品、非法种植罂粟、大麻等植物、引诱、教唆他人吸食、注射毒品等，都作了相应的处罚规定。

7. 依次填入下面一段文字横线处的语句，衔接最恰当的是哪一组？

铁路客车动车组先进的计算机网络控制技术，____，____，____，____，____。列车防火系统也很先进，重要设施都附有防火装置。

①并与地面通讯，实现地面对列车的监控

②能实现对动车组各个系统的控制

③一旦出现异常情况，动车组即可自动减速或停车

④同时对系统进行监视和故障诊断

⑤无须人为干预

A. ②①⑤④③　　B. ②④①③⑤　　C. ⑤④③②①　　D. ⑤④①③②

8. 依次填入下列空格中的人物，哪一项是准确的？

《三国演义》中塑造了一系列形象鲜明、个性突出的人物，有仁爱诚义、三顾

茅庐的君主______，有义勇傲慢、夜读《春秋》的猛将______，有刚愎自用、失守街亭的______，有贪功冒进、身死落凤坡的______，有割发代首、宁负天下人的奸臣______。

A. 刘备　吕布　张飞　周瑜　司马懿　　B. 曹操　关羽　马谡　庞统　刘备
C. 刘备　关羽　马谡　庞统　曹操　　D. 孙权　周瑜　黄忠　庞统　曹操

9. 下列文化常识表述无误的是哪一项？
A. “四书”和“五经”曾在唐代合称为“九经”。
B. 周文王、周武王、周公、孔子、秦始皇、汉高祖、汉武帝被儒家尊称为圣人。
C. 从姓名可知，下面三兄弟按从大到小的排序应是：泰伯、虞仲、季历。
D. “戊申晦，五鼓”中的“晦”指的是农历的每月初一，“五鼓”指的是早上5点到7点。

10. 下列哪一项没有使用修辞手法？
A. 鲁迅的骨头是最硬的，他没有丝毫的奴颜和媚骨，这是殖民地半殖民地人民最可宝贵的性格。
B. 意象好比细微的水珠，意境则是飘浮于天上的云。
C. 传递你的微笑，传递你的友善，传递你的热情……世界会因此而不同。
D. 云是由水珠聚集而成的，但水珠一旦凝聚为云，则有了云的千姿百态。

（二）判断题（判断下列各题所表述的意思是否正确。如果正确，请在答题卡上与题号相对应的答题框选择填涂“T”，如果错误，则填涂“F”。每题1分，共5分）

11. 风、雅、颂、赋、比、兴合称为“《诗经》六义”。
12. “苗”是会意字，“妨”是形声字，“本”是指事字，“水”是象形字。
13. 《红楼梦》描述了贾、王、史、薛四大家族的兴衰荣辱以及贾宝玉和林黛玉、薛宝钗、妙玉、史湘云、晴雯等众多女子间的爱情悲剧。
14. “树开花了”中的“花”使用的是“花”字的本义，“眼睛花了”中的“花”使用的是“花”字的引申义，“逐鹿中原，花落谁家”中的“花”使用的是“花”的比喻义。
15. 契诃夫是享誉世界的短篇小说大师，代表作有《死魂灵》、《装在套子里的人》、《变色龙》等。

【非选择题】

（三）填空题（每空1分，共3分）

16. ________________，达则兼济天下。（《孟子·尽心上》）
17. 穷且益坚，________________。（王勃《滕王阁序》）
18. ____________________，千金散尽还复来。（李白《将进酒》）

二、阅读理解

（本题分选择题、非选择题两大部分。选择题的答案请填涂在答题卡上“选择题区”与题号、答案相对应的方框中；非选择题的答案则请填写在答题卡“非选择题答题区”中与题号相对应的位置上。共42分）

（一）现代文阅读（12分）

阅读下面的现代文，然后依题目要求把答案填涂或填写在答题卡上。

学问与趣味

梁实秋

前辈的学者常以学问的趣味启迪后生，因为他们自己实在是得到了学问的趣味，故不惜现身说法，诱导后学，使他们也在愉快的心情之下走进学问的大门。例如，梁任公先生就说过：“我是个主张趣味主义的人，倘若用化学分解‘梁启超’这件东西，把里头所含一种元素名叫‘趣味’的抽出来，只怕所剩下的仅有个零了。”任公先生注重趣味，学问甚是渊博，而并不存有任何外在的东西，只是“无所为而为”，故能有他那样的成就。一个人在学问上果能感觉到趣味，有时真会像是着了魔一般，真能废寝忘食，真能不知老之将至，苦苦钻研，锲而不舍，在学问上焉能不有收获？不过我常想，以任公先生而论，他后期的著述如历史研究法，先秦政治思想史，以及有关墨子佛学陶渊明的作品，都可说是他的一点“趣味”在驱使着他，可是在他年青的时候，从师受业，诵读典籍，那时节也全然是趣味么？作八股文，作试帖诗，莫非也是趣味么？我想未必。大概趣味云云，是指年长之后自动做学问之时而言，在年青时候为学问打根底之际恐怕不能过分重视趣味。学问没有根底，趣味也很难滋生。任公先生的学问之所以那样的博大精深，涉笔成趣，左右逢源，不能不说一大部分得力于他的学问根底之打得坚固。

我曾见许多年青的朋友，聪明用功，成绩优异，而语文程度不足以达意，甚至写一封信亦难得通顺，问其故则曰其兴趣不在语文方面。又有一些人，执笔为文，斐然可诵，而视数理科目如仇，勉强才能及格，问其故则曰其兴趣不在数理方面，而且他们觉得某些科目没有趣味，便撇在一旁视如敝屣，怡然自得，振振有词，略无愧色，好像这就是发扬趣味主义。殊不知天下没有趣味的学问，端视吾人如何发掘其趣味，如果在良师指导之下按部就班的循序而进，一步一步地发现新天地，当然乐在其中，如果浅尝辄止，甚至躐等躁进，当然味同嚼蜡，自讨没趣。一个有中上天资的人，对于普通的基本的文理科目，都同样的有学习的能力，绝不会本能的长于此而拙于彼。只有懒惰与任性，才能使一个人自甘暴弃地在“趣味”的掩护之下败退。

由小学到中学，所修习的无非是一些普通的基本知识。就是大学四年，所授课业也还是相当粗浅的学识。世人常称大学为“最高学府”，这名称易滋误解，好像过此以上即无学问可言。大学的研究所才是初步研究学问的所在，在这里做学问也只能算是粗涉藩篱，注重的是研究学问的方法与实习。学无止境，一生的时间都嫌太短，所以古人皓首穷经，头发白了还是在继续研究，不过在这样的研究中确是有浓厚的趣味。

在初学的阶段，由小学到大学，我们与其倡言趣味，不如偏重纪律。一个合理编列的课程表，犹如一个营养均衡的食谱，里面各个项目都是有益而必需的，不可偏废，不可再有选择。所谓选修科目也只是在某一项目范围内略有拣选余地而已。一个受过良好教育的人，犹如一个科班出身的戏剧演员，在坐科的时候他是要服从严格纪律的，唱工做工武把子都要认真学习，各种角色的戏都要完全谙通，学成之后才能各按其趣味而单独发展其所长。学问要有根底，根底要打得平正坚实，以后永远受用。初学阶段的科目之最重要的莫过于语文与数学。语文是阅读达意的工具，国文不通便很难表达自己，外国文不通便很难吸取外来的新知。数学是思想条理之最好的训练。其他科目也各有各的用处，其重要性很难强分轩轾。例如体育，从另一方面看也是重要得无以复加。总之，我们在求学时代，应该暂且把趣味放在一旁，耐着性子接受教育的纪律，把自己锻炼成为坚实的材料。学问的趣味，留在将来慢慢享受一点也不迟。

【选择题】

（本题为单项选择题，每题 3 分，共 12 分）

19. 下列说法哪一项是正确的？

A. 作者认为梁任公所说的话错误不少，并不足信。

B. 作者认为只有打下学问的根底，做学问才能有趣味。

C. 梁任公认为做学问只能凭趣味，没有趣味是做不好学问的。

D. 梁任公与普通人不一样，做学问全靠趣味，而普通人则应主要靠根底。

20. 下列说法哪一项是正确的？

A. 文章称赞梁任公凭趣味做学问，期待读者以梁任公为榜样，做学问时追求趣味。

B. 文章写梁任公是为了论述趣味对做学问的重要性。

C. 文章写梁任公是为了论述根底对做学问的重要性。

D. 文章写梁任公是为了论述根底在做学问中具有与趣味同等的重要性。

21. “只有懒惰与任性，才能使一个人自甘暴弃地在‘趣味’的掩护之下败退”属于哪一种复句类型？

A. 条件复句　B. 假设复句　C. 递进复句　D. 承接复句

22. 下列哪一说法与原文意思不符？

A. 作者认为语文是最重要的学科之一，即使没有兴趣也应学好。

B. 作者认为在大学及之前，根底比趣味更重要。

C. 作者希望想做学问的学生要重视根底，而打根底很可能会缺乏趣味。

D. 作者认为大学及之前的求学阶段要把趣味的学科暂且搁在一边，优先学习那些没有趣味的学科。

（二）文言文阅读（30分）
阅读下面的文章或诗词，然后依题目要求把答案填涂或填写在答题卡上。
阅读材料一：

魏有隐士曰侯嬴，年七十，家贫，为大梁夷门监者。公子闻之，往请，欲厚遗之，不肯受，曰："臣修身洁行数十年，终不以监门困故而受公子财。"公子于是乃置酒大会宾客。坐定，公子从车骑，虚左，自迎夷门侯生。侯生摄敝衣冠，直上载公子上坐，不让，欲以观公子。公子执辔愈恭。侯生又谓公子曰："臣有客在市屠中，愿枉车骑过之。"公子引车入市。侯生下，见其客朱亥，俾倪，故久立与其客语。微察公子，公子颜色愈和。当是时，魏将相宗室宾客满堂，待公子举酒；市人皆观公子执辔，从骑皆窃骂侯生。侯生视公子色终不变，乃谢客就车。至家，公子引侯生坐上坐，遍赞宾客，宾客皆惊。酒酣，公子起，为寿侯生前。侯生因谓公子曰："今日嬴之为公子亦足矣！嬴乃夷门抱关者也，而公子亲枉车骑自迎嬴。于众人广坐之中，不宜有所过，今公子故过之。然嬴欲就公子之名，故久立公子车骑市中，过客，以观公子，公子愈恭。市人皆以嬴为小人，而以公子为长者，能下士也。"

于是罢酒，侯生遂为上客。

侯生谓公子曰："臣所过屠者朱亥，此子贤者，世莫能知，故隐屠间耳。"公子往，数请之，朱亥故不复谢。公子怪之。

阅读材料二：

秦士录

宋　濂

邓弼，秦人也，身长七尺，能以力雄人。邻牛方斗不可擘，拳其脊，折仆地。然好使酒，怒视人，人见辄避，曰："狂生不可近，近则必得奇辱。"

一日，独饮娼楼，两书生过其下，急牵入共饮。两生素贱其人，力拒之。弼怒曰："君终不我从，必杀君，亡命走山泽耳，不能忍君苦也！"两生不得已，从之。酒酣，解衣箕踞。两生雅闻其酒狂，欲起走，弼止之曰："勿走也！今日非速君饮，欲少吐胸中不平气耳。四库书从君问，即不能答，当血是刃。"两生遽摘"七经"数十义扣之，弼历举传疏，不遗一言。弼笑曰："君等伏乎未也？"两生不敢再有问。弼被发跳叫曰："古者学在养气，今人一服儒衣，反奄奄欲绝，徒欲驰骋文墨，儿抚一世豪杰。此何可哉！君等休矣。"两生素负多才艺，闻弼言，大愧。归，询其所与游，亦未尝见其挟册呻吟也。

泰定末，德王执法西御史台，弼造书数千言，袖谒之。阍卒不为通，弼连击踣数人，王令隶人捽入。弼盛气曰："公奈何不礼壮士？今天下虽号无事，东海岛夷，尚未臣顺；西南诸蛮，虽曰称臣奉贡，而称制与中国等。诚得如弼者一二辈，驱十万横磨剑伐之，则东西为日所出入，莫非王土矣。公奈何不礼壮士！"王曰："尔自号壮士，百万军中，可刺大将乎？"曰："能。"王曰："姑试之。"阴戒善槊者五十人，驰马出东门外。暨弼至，众槊齐进，弼虎吼而奔，人马辟易五十步。已而烟尘涨天，但见双剑飞舞，连斫马首堕地。王抚髀欢曰："诚壮士！诚壮士！"乃命勺酒劳弼，弼立饮不拜。

王上章荐诸天子，会丞相与王有隙，格其事不下。弼叹曰："天生一具铜筋铁肋，不使立勋万里外，乃槁死三尺蒿下，命也，亦时也。尚何言！"遂入王屋山为道士，后十年终。

史官曰：弼死未二十年，天下大乱，中原数千里，人影殆绝。玄鸟来降，失家，竟栖林木间。使弼在，必当有以自见，惜哉！弼鬼不灵则已，若有灵，吾知其怒发上冲也。

（本文有删节）

阅读材料三：

少年游·早行

林 仰

雾霞散晓月犹明，疏木挂残星。山径人稀，翠萝深处，啼鸟两三声。
霜华重迫驼裘冷，心共马蹄轻。十里青山，一溪流水，都做许多情。

【选择题】

（本题为单项选择题，每题 3 分，共 21 分）

23. 材料一中的下列句子里，加方框的词意思相同的是哪一组？

A. 于众人广坐之中，不宜有所过，今公子故过之　　过客，以观公子

B. 故久立与其客语　　故久立公子车骑市中

C. 终不以监门困故而受公子财　　今公子故过之

D. 乃谢客就车　　朱亥故不复谢

24. 在材料一中，侯生下列行为全都不属于对信陵君进行考验的是哪一组？

①侯生摄敝衣冠，直上载公子上坐，不让。

②公子引车入市，侯生下，见其客朱亥，俾倪，故久立与其客语。

③不肯受，曰："臣修身洁行数十年，终不以监门困故而受公子财。"

④侯生谓公子曰："臣所过屠者朱亥，此子贤者，世莫能知，故隐屠间耳。"公子往，数请之，朱亥故不复谢。

⑤侯生视公子色终不变，乃谢客就车。

A. ①②　　B. ②③⑤　　C. ③④⑤　　D. ①④⑤

25. 下列的说法中，与材料一原文意思相符的是哪一项？

A. 信陵君选择侯生生日这一天大宴宾客，以示对侯生的尊重。

B. 信陵君不辞辛劳，亲自到梁国去迎接侯生，足见其诚意。

C. 信陵君地位比侯生高，年龄也比侯生大，却非常尊重侯生，侯生因此被感动而

愿为其效力。

D. 侯生、朱亥都对信陵君有不尊重之处，但信陵君均不计较。

26. 对材料二中下列句子加方框的词的解释，不正确的是哪一项？

A. 两生素[贱]其人，力拒之　　贱：鄙视

B. 今日非[速]君饮，欲少吐胸中不平气耳　　速：邀请

C. 两生素[负]多才艺，闻弼言，大愧　　负：享有

D. 询其所与[游]，亦未尝见其挟册呻吟也　　游：交往

27. 材料二中下列各组句子里，加方框的词的意义和用法都相同的是哪一组？

A. ①两生雅闻[其]酒狂，欲起走　　②询[其]所与游，亦未尝见其挟册呻吟也

B. ①此[何]可哉！君等休矣　　②命也，亦时也。尚[何]言

C. ①虽曰称臣奉贡，[而]称制与中国等　　②弼虎吼[而]奔，人马辟易五十步

D. ①[乃]命匀酒劳弼，弼立饮不拜　　②不使立勋万里外，[乃]槁死三尺蒿下

28. 在材料二中，下列省略句括弧中所补的省略成分，正确的是哪一项？

A. 邻牛方斗不可擘，拳其脊，（弼）折仆地

B. 弼造书数千言，袖谒之。阍卒不为（王）通

C. 徒欲驰骋文墨，（两书生）儿抚一世豪杰

D. （弼）天生一具铜筋铁肋，不使（弼）立勋（于）万里外

29. 下面是对材料二有关内容的分析和概括，不正确的是哪一项？

A. 邓弼，秦地人，身材高大，力气极大，而且嗜好喝酒，常常借酒使性，羞辱旁人，因此大家看见他就都远远地躲避开。

B. 邓弼强拉两位儒生到娼楼喝酒，并与他俩比试学问。邓弼博通经传，让两儒生非常羞愧，自此他俩再也不敢拿书吟诵。

C. 邓弼带着文稿，强闯德王府，建议德王要居安思危，礼贤下士，并指出，若能这样做，就能安抚边夷，天下皆为王土。

D. 德王向朝廷举荐邓弼，但丞相与德王不和，便从中作梗阻止。邓弼因此悲叹自己生不逢时，壮志难酬，于是遁迹山林。

【非选择题】

（本题为翻译题或简答题，共 9 分）

30. 翻译材料一中的文句“公子往，数请之，朱亥故不复谢。公子怪之”。(3 分)

31. 在材料三中，词的题目为“早行”，词人在上阕是如何表现“早”的？(2 分)

32. 在材料三中，词的下阕表现了诗人怎样的心境？又是如何表现的？请结合词句简要赏析。(4 分)

三、语言文字表达（共70分）

33. 给下面寓言补写一段结尾，要求：(1) 注重心理活动描写；(2) 既出人意料，又合乎情理。(40字左右，10分)

在众多的兔姐妹中，有一只白兔独具审美的慧心。她爱大自然的美，尤爱皎洁的月色。每天夜晚，她来到林中草地，一边无忧无虑地嬉戏，一边心旷神怡地赏月。她不愧是赏月的行家，在她的眼里，月的阴晴圆缺无不各具风韵。在众姐妹的眼里，她是高雅的象征，是诗意的化身，是圣洁的使者，是世间的女神。

于是，天帝召见这只白兔，向她宣布了一个慷慨的决定："万物均有所归属。从今以后，月亮归属于你，因为你的赏月之才举世无双。"

白兔仍然夜夜到林中草地赏月。

可是，说也奇怪，____

____

34. 请从下列两题中任选一题写一篇作文，体裁不限，诗歌除外。现代文要求不少于700字，文言文不少于400字。(60分)

题一：人与人存在天然的差异，后天的努力可能缩小这种差异，也可能扩大这种差异；但是人类又坚信"人生而平等"的道德理念。你如何理解人与人的"平等"与"差异"？请以"平等与差异"为话题，自拟题目写一篇作文。

题二：请以"人生的选择"为题写一篇作文。

暨南大学、华侨大学联合招收港澳地区、台湾省、华侨、华人及其他外籍学生入学考试样题

中国语文
答题卡

选择题区			
	1 [A] [B] [C] [D]	6 [A] [B] [C] [D]	11 [T] [F]
	2 [A] [B] [C] [D]	7 [A] [B] [C] [D]	12 [T] [F]
	3 [A] [B] [C] [D]	8 [A] [B] [C] [D]	13 [T] [F]
	4 [A] [B] [C] [D]	9 [A] [B] [C] [D]	14 [T] [F]
	5 [A] [B] [C] [D]	10 [A] [B] [C] [D]	15 [T] [F]
	19 [A] [B] [C] [D]	23 [A] [B] [C] [D]	27 [A] [B] [C] [D]
	20 [A] [B] [C] [D]	24 [A] [B] [C] [D]	28 [A] [B] [C] [D]
	21 [A] [B] [C] [D]	25 [A] [B] [C] [D]	29 [A] [B] [C] [D]
	22 [A] [B] [C] [D]	26 [A] [B] [C] [D]	

以下为非选择题答题区，必须用黑色字迹的钢笔或签字笔在指定的黑色区域内作答，否则答案无效。

一、基础知识

（二）填空题

16. ______________________________

17. ______________________________

18. ______________________________

二、阅读理解

现代文阅读 19 ~ 22 题请在“选择题区”填涂答案；文言文阅读 23 ~ 29 题请在“选择题区”填涂答案。

30. 译文：______________________________

____

31. ______________________________

32. ______________________________

____

三、语言文字表达

33. ______________________________

____

34. 作文（略）

中国语文参考答案

一、基础知识（38 分）

（一）单项选择题（共 10 题，每题 3 分，共 30 分）

1. D　（A 项，祥、身；B 项，律、吁；C 项，缉、极）
2. C　因果倒置，“所以”改为“因为”。
3. A　①中应选“年轻”。“年轻”指人的岁数不大，有相比较而言之义：他很年轻/我比他年轻/领导班子年轻化；而“年青”则为处于青年时期，不合语境。②中应选“以至”。“以至”有“一直到”的意思，表示时间、数量、程度、范围等的延伸；而“以致”是“因而导致”的意思，后面接的往往是不好的结果。“踌躇满志”是中性词，形容对自己取得的成就非常得意；而“自鸣得意”是贬义词，自以为了不起。
4. C　胶柱鼓瑟：比喻固执拘泥，不能变通。（A 项河东狮吼：比喻妇人妒悍，大吵大闹。B 项久假不归：长时间借去不归还。D 项气宇轩昂：形容人气度非凡）
5. D　（A 项成分残缺，由于句首的状语淹没了主语，导致谓语“引起”缺失了陈述的对象；B 项结构混乱，前一句的主语是“学生”，后一句的主语却暗换成了“考场满分作文”；C 项搭配不当，“执掌”与“主教练”不搭配）
6. B　这分号用得正确，这是全句中最大的停顿，而前后又是并列关系。（A 项最后的问号应改为句号，因为整个句子是陈述语气。C 项冒号应改为逗号，因为前后都是省领导说的话，说话人在中间。D 项错用顿号，混淆了大小并列的界限。“持有毒品”和“大麻等植物”后的顿号都应改为逗号）
7. B　8. C
9. C　“四书”是南宋朱熹首次提出的。
10. D

（二）判断题（每题 1 分，共 5 分）

11. T　12. T
13. F　（贾宝玉只与林黛玉相恋，与其他女子只是亲情或友情，而没有爱情）
14. T
15. F　（《死魂灵》是果戈理的长篇小说）

（三）填空题（每空 1 分，共 3 分）

16. 穷则独善其身
17. 不坠青云之志
18. 人生得意须尽欢

二、阅读理解（共 42 分）

（一）现代文阅读（每题 3 分，共 12 分）

19. B　20. C　21. A　22. D

（二）文言文阅读（其中选择题 21 分，非选择题 9 分，共 30 分）

23. A　（B 项前一个是侯生故久立，后一个是故意使公子车骑久立；C 项前一个故是原因，后一个是特意的意思；D 项前一个谢是告辞，后一个是回访）

24. C　侯生不受钱财，是表明自己的品行；侯生推荐朱亥是开始为信陵君效力；侯生上车是考验满意后的行为，非考验本身。

25. D　“为寿”是祝酒，并庆寿；“大梁”是魏都，非国名；“长者”指地位高，非年龄大。

26. C　负是“自恃”。

27. A　①②均为人称代词，指邓弼。（B 项①疑问副词，“怎么”；②疑问代词，“什么”。C 项①连词，表转折，“却”；②连词，表修饰。D 项①副词，表顺接，“于是”；②副词，表逆接，“竟”）

28. D　（A 项应为“邻牛”脊折仆地。B 项应不为“邓弼”通报。C 项应为“今之儒生”）

29. B　原文是“归，询其所与游，亦未尝见其挟册呻吟也”。意思是说：两书生回家后，询问与邓弼交往的人，大家都说从未见过邓弼拿书本吟诵。

30. 译文：公子拜访朱亥，多次请他，朱亥故意不回拜，公子觉得他很奇怪。（“数”1 分，“谢”1 分，“怪”1 分）

31. 诗人是用“霁霞”、“晓月”、“残星”、行人稀少的山径和啼鸟声等意象（景物）来表现“早”的。（意思答对即可，2 分）

32. 表现了词人轻松愉快的心境（2 分）。通过“心共马蹄轻”直接写轻快愉悦（1 分），也通过拟人的手法来写青山流水皆有情（1 分）。

三、语言文字表达（共 70 分）

33. 在续写时，要特别注意与“说也奇怪”相一致。（40 字左右，10 分）

34. 作文（60 分）（略）

数　学

考试要求

数学科主要考查考生能否正确理解和掌握初等数学的基础知识和基本思想方法，能否熟练运用本大纲规定范围内的数学知识和数学思想方法分析问题、解决问题。

考试范围与内容

一、代数

1. 代数式

   整式、分式及其运算，因式分解，余数定理，因式定理；根式及其运算，二次根式的有理化。

2. 集合

   集合、子集、交集、并集、全集、补集。

3. 方程

   一元二次方程的解法，一元二次方程根的判别式，根与系数的关系（韦达定理）；分式方程的解法，简单无理方程的解法；二元一次联立方程组的解法。

4. 不等式

   不等式及其性质；一元一次不等式、一元一次不等式组、一元二次不等式的解法，含绝对值的不等式的解法；平均值不等式。

5. 函数

   函数的定义，函数的表示法，函数的单调性、奇偶性、周期性，反函数，互为反函数的函数以及它们的图像之间的关系。

6. 几种常见的函数

   正比例函数、反比例函数、一次函数、二次函数、幂函数的定义、图像和性质；指数、对数的定义及其运算性质；指数函数、对数函数的定义、图像和性质；解简单的指数方程和对数方程，解简单的指数不等式和对数不等式。

7. 数列

   数列的基本概念，等差数列、等比数列；求数列的通项公式与前 n 项和公式。

二、三角

1. 角的有关概念

角的定义（正角、负角、零角、象限角），角的度量（角度制、弧度制）。

2. 任意角的三角函数

三角函数的定义（正弦、余弦、正切、余切）；特殊角的三角函数值；同角三角函数的基本关系，三角函数的诱导公式，两角和与差的正弦、余弦、正切，二倍角的正弦、余弦、正切。

3. 三角函数的图像和性质

正弦函数、余弦函数、正切函数的图像和性质（周期性、单调性、奇偶性、最大值与最小值）；已知三角函数值求角。

4. 解三角形

勾股定理，解直角三角形；正弦定理，余弦定理，解斜三角形。

三、平面解析几何

1. 直线

直线的倾斜角与斜率，直线方程的各种形式（点斜式、斜截式、两点式、截距式、一般式）；两条直线的位置关系，点到直线的距离，两条直线的交点，两条相交直线的夹角。

2. 圆

圆的标准方程和一般方程，直线与圆的位置关系。

3. 圆锥曲线

椭圆、双曲线、抛物线的定义、标准方程和简单几何性质。

四、立体几何

1. 空间直线与平面

平面及其基本性质，平行直线，异面直线；直线与平面平行、平面与平面平行、直线与平面垂直、平面与平面垂直的判定与性质；三垂线定理及其逆定理。

2. 夹角与距离

异面直线的夹角，直线与平面所成的角，二面角及其平面角；点到平面的距离，直线到与它平行的平面的距离，两个平行平面的距离。

五、概率初步

1. 排列、组合与二项式定理

分类计数原理（加法原理）与分步计数原理（乘法原理）；排列与排列数，组合与组合数，排列、组合的简单应用；二项式定理。

2. 概率初步

随机事件的概率，等可能事件的概率，互斥事件有一个发生的概率，相互独立事件同时发生的概率，独立重复试验。

考试形式

考试采用闭卷、书面作答形式，试卷满分为 150 分，考试时间为 120 分钟。

试卷结构与题型

试卷包括选择题、填空题和解答题三种题型。选择题为四选一型的单项选择题；填空题只要求直接填写结果，不要求写出计算或推证过程；解答题包括计算题、证明题和应用题等类型，解答应写出文字说明、演算步骤或推证过程。

试卷各种比例关系如下：

（1）各部分内容所占比例：

代数	约 45%
三角	约 18%
平面解析几何	约 20%
立体几何	约 5%
概率初步	约 12%

（2）各种题型所占分数：

选择题	60 分
填空题	30 分
解答题	60 分

考生复习参考资料

1. 赖章荣. 暨南大学、华侨大学联合招收港澳地区、台湾省、华侨、华人及其他外籍学生入学考试复习丛书 · 数学. 广州：暨南大学出版社，2015.
2. 赖章荣. 暨南大学、华侨大学两校联招及全国联招 2004—2011 年试题详解丛书 · 数学. 广州：暨南大学出版社，2013.
3. 赖章荣. 暨南大学、华侨大学及全国联招考试模拟试题丛书 · 数学. 广州：暨南大学出版社，2013.

样卷

暨南大学、华侨大学联合招收港澳地区、台湾省、华侨、华人及其他外籍学生入学考试样题

科目：数　学

答卷时间：120 分钟

一、选择题（本大题共 15 小题，每小题 4 分，共 60 分。每小题所列四个选项中只有一个是正确的，请把你的选择按题号填入答题纸）

1. 已知集合 $A=\{x|x>1\}$，$B=\{x|-1\leqslant x\leqslant 2\}$，则 $A\cup B=$

A. $\{x|x\geqslant -1\}$　　B. $\{x|x\leqslant 2\}$　　C. $\{x|0<x\leqslant 2\}$　　D. $\{x|-1\leqslant x\leqslant 2\}$

2. 已知函数 $f(x)=5x-7$，则 $f(f(2))=$

A. 10　　B. 8　　C. 6　　D. 12

3. 已知 $a=\log_4 5$，$b=\log_5 64$，则 $a\cdot b$ 的值为

A. 3　　B. 2　　C. $\frac{1}{3}$　　D. $\frac{1}{2}$

4. 直线 $2x+\sqrt{3}y-1=0$ 的斜率是

A. $-\frac{\sqrt{3}}{2}$　　B. $\frac{\sqrt{3}}{2}$　　C. $-\frac{2\sqrt{3}}{3}$　　D. $\frac{2\sqrt{3}}{3}$

5. 以 $A(0,1)$、$B(2,3)$ 为直径两端的圆与 y 轴的另一个交点是

A. $(0,-1)$　　B. $(0,2)$　　C. $(0,3)$　　D. $(0,4)$

6. 函数 $y=4x+7$ $(x\in\mathrm{R})$ 的反函数是

A. $y=-\frac{x-7}{4}$ $(x\in\mathrm{R})$　　B. $y=\frac{x+7}{4}$ $(x\in\mathrm{R})$

C. $y=-\frac{x+7}{4}$ $(x\in\mathrm{R})$　　D. $y=\frac{x-7}{4}$ $(x\in\mathrm{R})$

7. 在等差数列 $\{a_n\}$ 中，已知它的前 20 项之和为 420，则 $a_9+a_{12}=$

A. 25　　B. 40　　C. 36　　D. 42

8. 下列函数中，既是奇函数又是增函数的是

A. $y=\sin 5x$　　B. $y=x^{\frac{1}{3}}$　　C. $y=x^{-\frac{1}{2}}$　　D. $y=\log_3 x$

9. 已知不等式 $x^2+2x+a<0$ 的解集为 $\{x|-4<x<2\}$，则实数 a 的值是

A. 8　　B. -8　　C. 6　　D. -6

10. 函数 $y=\sin^2 x+2\cos^2 x-4\cos x+5$ 的最大值是

A. 11　　B. 10　　C. 5　　D. 4

11. 下列命题中正确的是

A. 空间中，垂直于同一条直线的两直线平行

B. 空间中，垂直于同一个平面的两直线平行

C. 空间中，垂直于同一个平面的两平面平行

D. 空间中，与同一个平面所成的角相等的两直线平行

12. 在$\triangle ABC$中，$AB=AC=5$，$BC=6$，$PA\perp$平面ABC，$PA=8$，则P到BC的距离是

A. $\sqrt{5}$　　B. $2\sqrt{5}$　　C. $3\sqrt{5}$　　D. $4\sqrt{5}$

13. 三角形ABC中，内角A、B、C所对的边分别为a、b、c，如果$C=30°$，$a=20$，$\sin A=\frac{1}{3}$，那么$c=$

A. 20　　B. 40　　C. 10　　D. 30

14. 同时掷两颗质地均匀的骰子（六个面分别标有1～6个点的正方体），两颗骰子向上面的点数之和为5的概率是

A. $\frac{1}{9}$　　B. $\frac{1}{10}$　　C. $\frac{1}{8}$　　D. $\frac{1}{6}$

15. 在包括甲、乙在内的6人中选出4人排成一排，若甲、乙不全选出，则不同的排法共有

A. 144种　　B. 216种　　C. 336种　　D. 360种

二、填空题（本大题共6小题，每小题5分，共30分。请把答案按题号填入答题纸）

16. 不等式$\sqrt{x-5}\leqslant 8$的解集是________________。

17. 函数$y=\frac{x^2-2x+4}{x}$（$x>0$）的最小值是________。

18. 已知$\tan\alpha=7$，则$\sin 2\alpha$的值为________。

19. 已知抛物线$y^2=2px$（$p>0$）的焦点恰好为双曲线$x^2-y^2=2$的一个焦点，则p的值为________。

20. 从1，2，3，4，5，6，7，8，9，10这10个数中任取3个数，则取出的3个数之和为奇数的取法共有________种。（用数字作答）

21. 甲、乙两台机床制造同一种零件，甲机床的废品率为0.04，乙机床的废品率为0.05，从它们制造的零件中各任取1件，其中恰有1件废品的概率是________。（用数字作答）

三、解答题（本大题共4小题，每小题15分，共60分。解答应写出文字说明、证明过程或演算步骤，请把你的解答按题号写在答题纸上）

22. 已知函数$f(x)=x^2+\frac{a}{x}$（$x\neq 0$，$a\in\mathbf{R}$）。

（1）判断函数$f(x)$的奇偶性；

（2）若$f(x)$在区间$[2,+\infty)$是增函数，求实数a的取值范围。

23. 在$\triangle ABC$中，内角A、B、C所对的边分别为a、b、c，已知$\frac{\cos A-2\cos C}{\cos B}=\frac{2c-a}{b}$。

（1）求$\frac{\sin C}{\sin A}$的值；

（2）若$\cos B=\frac{1}{4}$，$b=2$，求a的值。

24. （选考历史或地理的考生做题目Ⅰ，不必做题目Ⅱ；选考物理、化学或生物的考生做题目Ⅱ，不必做题目Ⅰ）

Ⅰ. 设数列$\{a_n\}$的前n项和为S_n，已知$a_1+2a_2+3a_3+\cdots+na_n=(n-1)S_n+2n$（$n=1, 2, 3, \cdots$）。

（1）求a_2、a_3的值；

（2）求证：数列$\{S_n+2\}$是等比数列。

Ⅱ. 记等比数列$\{a_n\}$的前n项和为S_n，已知对任意正整数n，点（n，S_n）均在以x为自变量的函数$y=b^x+r$（b、r均为实常数，且$b>0$，$b\neq 1$）的图像上。

（1）求r的值；

（2）当$b=2$时，记$b_n=\frac{n+1}{4a_n}$（$n=1, 2, 3, \cdots$），求数列$\{b_n\}$的前n项和T_n。

25. （选考历史或地理的考生做题目Ⅰ，不必做题目Ⅱ；选考物理、化学或生物的考生做题目Ⅱ，不必做题目Ⅰ）

Ⅰ. 设F_1、F_2分别是椭圆C：$\frac{x^2}{a^2}+\frac{y^2}{b^2}=1$（$a>b>0$）的左、右焦点。

（1）设椭圆C上的点（$\sqrt{3}$，$\frac{\sqrt{3}}{2}$）到F_1、F_2两点的距离之和等于4，写出椭圆C的方程和焦点坐标；

（2）设点P是椭圆C上任意一点，过原点的直线l与椭圆相交于M、N两点，当直线PM、PN的斜率都存在，且分别为k_1、k_2时，$k_1\cdot k_2$的值是否与点P的位置及直线l的斜率有关？证明你的结论。

Ⅱ. 已知椭圆C：$\frac{x^2}{a^2}+\frac{y^2}{b^2}=1$（$a>b>0$）的离心率为$\frac{1}{2}$，且经过点（1，$\frac{3}{2}$）。

（1）求椭圆C的方程和焦点坐标；

（2）已知A为椭圆C的左顶点，直线l过右焦点F且与椭圆C交于M，N两点，若AM、AN的斜率分别为k_1、k_2，且满足$k_1+k_2=m$（定值$m\neq 0$），求直线l的方程。

暨南大学、华侨大学联合招收港澳地区、台湾省、华侨、华人及其他外籍学生入学考试样题

数　学

答题卡

一、选择题

1 [A] [B] [C] [D]	6 [A] [B] [C] [D]	11 [A] [B] [C] [D]
2 [A] [B] [C] [D]	7 [A] [B] [C] [D]	12 [A] [B] [C] [D]
3 [A] [B] [C] [D]	8 [A] [B] [C] [D]	13 [A] [B] [C] [D]
4 [A] [B] [C] [D]	9 [A] [B] [C] [D]	14 [A] [B] [C] [D]
5 [A] [B] [C] [D]	10 [A] [B] [C] [D]	15 [A] [B] [C] [D]

以下为非选择题答题区，必须用黑色字迹的钢笔或签字笔在指定的黑色框区域内作答，否则答案无效。

二、填空题

16. ________________　17. ________________

18. ________________　19. ________________

20. ________________　21. ________________

三、解答题

22.

23.

24.（选考历史或地理的考生做题目Ⅰ，不必做题目Ⅱ；选考物理、化学或生物的考生做题目Ⅱ，不必做题目Ⅰ）

25.（选考历史或地理的考生做题目Ⅰ，不必做题目Ⅱ；选考物理、化学或生物的考生做题目Ⅱ，不必做题目Ⅰ）

数学参考答案

一、选择题（本大题共15小题，每小题4分，共60分）

1. A　2. B　3. A　4. C　5. C　6. D　7. D　8. B　9. B　10. A　11. B
12. D　13. D　14. A　15. B

二、填空题（本大题共6小题，每小题5分，共30分）

16. $\{x|5\leqslant x\leqslant 69\}$　17. 2　18. $\frac{7}{25}$　19. 4　20. 60　21. 0.086

三、解答题（本大题共4小题，每小题15分，共60分）

22. 解：（1）当 $a=0$ 时，$f(x)=x^2$，为偶函数；当 $a\neq 0$ 时，$f(x)$既不是奇函数也不是偶函数。

（2）设 $x_2>x_1\geqslant 2$，则 $f(x_1)-f(x_2)=x_1^2+\frac{a}{x_1}-x_2^2-\frac{a}{x_2}=\frac{x_1-x_2}{x_1x_2}[x_1x_2(x_1+x_2)-a]$，

由 $x_2>x_1\geqslant 2$ 得 $x_1x_2(x_1+x_2)>16$，$x_1-x_2<0$，$x_1x_2>0$，

要使$f(x)$在区间$[2,+\infty)$是增函数，只需$f(x_1)-f(x_2)<0$，

即 $x_1x_2(x_1+x_2)-a>0$ 恒成立，故得 $a\leqslant 16$。

23. 解：（1）由正弦定理得

$a=2R\sin A$，$b=2R\sin B$，$c=2R\sin C$，其中 R 为$\triangle ABC$ 的外接圆半径，

所以$\frac{\cos A-2\cos C}{\cos B}=\frac{2c-a}{b}=\frac{2\sin C-\sin A}{\sin B}$，

$\sin B\cos A-2\sin B\cos C=2\sin C\cos B-\sin A\cos B$，

$\sin(A+B)=2\sin(B+C)$，$\sin(\pi-C)=2\sin(\pi-A)$，

$\sin C=2\sin A$，所以$\frac{\sin C}{\sin A}=2$。

（2）由（1）知：$\frac{c}{a}=\frac{\sin C}{\sin A}=2$，即 $c=2a$，

又因为 $b=2$，故由余弦定理得：$b^2=a^2+c^2-2ac\cos B$，

即 $2^2=a^2+4a^2-2a\cdot 2a\cdot\frac{1}{4}$，

解得 $a=1$。

24. Ⅰ.（1）解：因为 $a_1+2a_2+3a_3+\cdots+na_n=(n-1)S_n+2n$（$n=1,2,3,\cdots$），

所以 $a_1=2$，$a_1+2a_2=(a_1+a_2)+4$，

$a_1+2a_2+3a_3=2(a_1+a_2+a_3)+6$，

由此可得 $a_2=4$，$a_3=8$。

（2）证明：因为 $a_1+2a_2+3a_3+\cdots+na_n=(n-1)S_n+2n\ (n=1, 2, 3, \cdots)$ ①

所以当 $n\geqslant 2$ 时，$a_1+2a_2+3a_3+\cdots+(n-1)a_{n-1}=(n-2)S_{n-1}+2(n-1)$ ②

①－②得 $na_n=n(S_n-S_{n-1})-S_n+2S_{n-1}+2=na_n-S_n+2S_{n-1}+2$，

故 $S_n=2S_{n-1}+2$，$S_n+2=2(S_{n-1}+2)$。

因为 $S_1+2=a_1+2=4\neq 0$，所以 $S_{n-1}+2\neq 0$，所以$\dfrac{S_n+2}{S_{n-1}+2}=2$，

从而 $\{S_n+2\}$ 是首项为 4、公比为 2 的等比数列。

Ⅱ. 解：（1）因为对任意正整数 n，点 (n, S_n) 均在函数 $y=b^x+r$ 的图像上，所以 $S_n=b^n+r$，

当 $n=1$ 时，$a_1=S_1=b+r$；

当 $n\geqslant 2$ 时，$a_n=S_n-S_{n-1}=b^n+r-(b^{n-1}+r)=b^n-b^{n-1}=(b-1)b^{n-1}$，

因为 $\{a_n\}$ 为等比数列，所以公比为 b，

再由 $a_2=a_1b=(b+r)b$ 和 $a_2=(b-1)b$ 得 $r=-1$。

（2）当 $b=2$ 时，$a_n=(b-1)b^{n-1}=2^{n-1}$，$b_n=\dfrac{n+1}{4a_n}=\dfrac{n+1}{4\times 2^{n-1}}=\dfrac{n+1}{2^{n+1}}$，

则 $T_n=\dfrac{2}{2^2}+\dfrac{3}{2^3}+\dfrac{4}{2^4}+\cdots+\dfrac{n+1}{2^{n+1}}$，

$\dfrac{1}{2}T_n=\dfrac{2}{2^3}+\dfrac{3}{2^4}+\dfrac{4}{2^5}+\cdots+\dfrac{n}{2^{n+1}}+\dfrac{n+1}{2^{n+2}}$，

上两式相减得：
$$\frac{1}{2}T_n=\frac{2}{2^2}+\frac{1}{2^3}+\frac{1}{2^4}+\frac{1}{2^5}+\cdots+\frac{1}{2^{n+1}}-\frac{n+1}{2^{n+2}}$$
$$=\frac{1}{2}+\frac{\frac{1}{2^3}\times\left(1-\frac{1}{2^{n-1}}\right)}{1-\frac{1}{2}}-\frac{n+1}{2^{n+2}}$$
$$=\frac{3}{4}-\frac{1}{2^{n+1}}-\frac{n+1}{2^{n+2}},$$

所以 $T_n=\dfrac{3}{2}-\dfrac{1}{2^n}-\dfrac{n+1}{2^{n+1}}=\dfrac{3}{2}-\dfrac{n+3}{2^{n+1}}$。

25. Ⅰ. 解：（1）由于点 $\left(\sqrt{3}, \dfrac{\sqrt{3}}{2}\right)$ 在椭圆上，故$\dfrac{(\sqrt{3})^2}{a^2}+\dfrac{\left(\frac{\sqrt{3}}{2}\right)^2}{b^2}=1$，

又因为点 $\left(\sqrt{3}, \dfrac{\sqrt{3}}{2}\right)$ 到 F_1、F_2 两点的距离之和等于 4，所以 $2a=4$，

所以 $a=2$，$b^2=3$，故椭圆 C 的方程为 $\dfrac{x^2}{4}+\dfrac{y^2}{3}=1$，

焦点坐标分别为（-1，0）、（1，0）。

（2）显然，过原点的直线 l 与椭圆相交的两点 M、N 关于坐标原点对称，设 M（x_0，y_0）、N（$-x_0$，$-y_0$）、P（x，y），因为点 M、N、P 在椭圆上，故有

$\frac{x_0^2}{a^2}+\frac{y_0^2}{b^2}=1$，$\frac{x^2}{a^2}+\frac{y^2}{b^2}=1$，两式相减并整理可得 $\frac{x^2-x_0^2}{a^2}+\frac{y^2-y_0^2}{b^2}=0$，

又 $k_1=\frac{y-y_0}{x-x_0}$，$k_2=\frac{y+y_0}{x+x_0}$，所以 $k_1\cdot k_2=\frac{y-y_0}{x-x_0}\cdot\frac{y+y_0}{x+x_0}=\frac{y^2-y_0^2}{x^2-x_0^2}=-\frac{b^2}{a^2}$，

这说明 $k_1\cdot k_2$ 的值与点 P 的位置无关，也与直线 l 的斜率无关。

Ⅱ．解：（1）因为 $e=\frac{c}{a}=\frac{1}{2}$，所以 $a=2c$，$b=\sqrt{a^2-c^2}=\sqrt{3}c$，

故椭圆方程为 $\frac{x^2}{4c^2}+\frac{y^2}{3c^2}=1$。

又椭圆经过点（1，$\frac{3}{2}$），所以 $\frac{1^2}{4c^2}+\frac{(\frac{3}{2})^2}{3c^2}=1$，

解得 $c=1$，

从而椭圆方程为 $\frac{x^2}{4}+\frac{y^2}{3}=1$，焦点坐标分别为（-1，0）、（1，0）。

（2）若直线 l 的斜率不存在，显然 $k_1+k_2=0$，不合题意，故直线 l 的斜率 k 必存在，因为直线 l 过右焦点 F（1，0），故直线 l 的方程为 $y=k(x-1)$，

设 M（x_1，y_1）、N（x_2，y_2），解方程组

$$\begin{cases}\frac{x^2}{4}+\frac{y^2}{3}=1\\ y=k(x-1)\end{cases},$$

得 $(3+4k^2)x^2-8k^2x+4k^2-12=0$，

由一元二次方程根与系数的关系得

$x_1+x_2=\frac{8k^2}{3+4k^2}$，$x_1\cdot x_2=\frac{4k^2-12}{3+4k^2}$，

因为点 A 的坐标为（-2，0），故

$$\begin{aligned}k_1+k_2&=\frac{y_1}{x_1+2}+\frac{y_2}{x_2+2}=k\left(\frac{x_1-1}{x_1+2}+\frac{x_2-1}{x_2+2}\right)\\&=k\left[2-3\left(\frac{1}{x_1+2}+\frac{1}{x_2+2}\right)\right]\\&=k\left[2-\frac{3(x_1+x_2+4)}{x_1x_2+2(x_1+x_2)+4}\right]\end{aligned}$$

$$=k\left[2-\frac{3\left(\frac{8k^2}{3+4k^2}+4\right)}{\frac{4k^2-12}{3+4k^2}+2\times\frac{8k^2}{3+4k^2}+4}\right]$$

$$=-\frac{1}{k},$$

由 $k_1+k_2=m$ 得 $k=-\frac{1}{m}$，从而直线 l 的方程为 $y=-\frac{1}{m}(x-1)$。

英　语

考试要求

命题遵循选拔性考试的规律与要求，在考查英语语言基础知识掌握和理解的同时，侧重考查考生在特定语言环境中运用语言完成任务的能力，命题以《暨南大学、华侨大学联合招收港澳地区、台湾省、华侨、华人及其他外籍学生入学考试复习大纲（2016—2020）》为依据。

考试范围与内容

一、语言知识

要求考生掌握并能运用英语语音、词汇和语法基础知识（如动词的时态和语态、动词不定式、动名词、分词、名词性从句、定语从句、状语从句、虚拟语气、倒装句等），要求掌握高中阶段所学的常用词及常用短语 3 500 个以上。

二、语言运用

1. 听力

要求考生能听懂日常话题的对话和简短独白。考生应能：

（1）理解主旨和要义；

（2）获取具体、事实性信息；

（3）对所听内容作出推断；

（4）理解说话者的意图、观点和态度。

2. 阅读

要求考生能读懂体裁多样、题材广泛的简短文段，如记叙文、说明文、议论文等，掌握一定的商务英语知识，并能从中获取相关信息。考生应能：

（1）理解文章的主旨和要义；

（2）理解文中具体信息；

（3）根据上下文推断生词的词义；

（4）作出判断和推理；

（5）理解文章的基本结构；

（6）理解作者的意图、观点和态度。

3. 单项选择题

要求考生掌握日常交际中的常用单词和固定短语，理解它们的意义和用法，熟练运用英语的语法基础知识，能在备选的四个选项中选出正确的答案。

4. 完形填空

在一篇题材熟悉、难易适中的短文（约200个词）中留有20个空格，每个空格为一题，每题四个选项。要求考生在全面理解内容的基础上选择最佳答案，目的在于测试考生综合运用语言的能力（包括语法、词语搭配和篇章理解等）。

5. 短文改错

要求考生在一篇短文的10个指定行中各找出一个错误，目的在于测试考生的语法知识及分析判断能力。

6. 填空题

要求考生在给定的12个单词中，依据句子结构的语法性和上下文连贯的要求，选出其中的10个单词填入空格内，注意使用词语的正确形式填空，每个单词仅能使用一次。其目的在于测试考生在具体语境中正确使用单词的能力（包括词义的理解、词语的搭配和词形的变化等）。

7. 写作

要求考生根据给定的要点或图表，写一篇150字左右的短文。要求考生能掌握一定的应用文写作技巧，能根据给定的情景正确表达思想，且意思连贯，无重大语法错误，能有效运用所学的语言知识。

考试形式

一、考查方式

（1）闭卷；

（2）听力和笔试。

二、笔试考试时间和分数

（1）时间：120分钟；

（2）分数：满分150分。

试卷结构与题型

一、试卷结构

（1）试卷分第一卷（选择题）和第二卷（非选择题）两部分；

（2）第一卷四部分，共110分；第二卷三部分，共40分。

二、题型

第一卷（选择题）

1. 听力理解 20 题，满分 30 分
   本部分包括两节：
   A 节（Section A）10 题，共 10 分；
   B 节（Section B）10 题，共 20 分。
2. 阅读理解 4 个篇章共 20 题，满分 40 分
3. 单项选择 20 题，满分 20 分
4. 完形填空 20 题，满分 20 分

第二卷（非选择题）

5. 短文改错 10 题，满分 10 分
6. 填空 10 题，满分 10 分
7. 写作 1 题，满分 20 分

考生复习参考资料

1. 陈芳. 暨南大学、华侨大学联合招收港澳地区、台湾省、华侨、华人及其他外籍学生入学考试复习丛书·英语. 广州：暨南大学出版社，2015.
2. 陈芳. 暨南大学、华侨大学及全国联招考试模拟试题丛书·英语. 广州：暨南大学出版社，2013.
3. 覃儒奎. 暨南大学、华侨大学两校联招及全国联招 2004—2011 年试题详解丛书·英语. 广州：暨南大学出版社，2013.

样卷

JINAN UNIVERSITY AND HUAQIAO UNIVERSITY

Entrance Examination
Sample Test

Subject：ENGLISH

本试卷分第一卷（选择题）和第二卷（非选择题）两部分。试卷满分为 150 分。考试时间为 120 分钟。

Paper Ⅰ（110 points）

Part I Listening Comprehension（30 points）

Directions：*In this section you will hear* 10 *short conversations between two speakers. At the end of each conversation, a third voice will ask a question about what was said. The conversation and the question will be spoken only once. After you hear a conversation and the question about it, read the four possible answers in your test paper and choose the best one to the question you have heard. Then, mark your answer by blackening the corresponding letter of your choice on the Answer Sheet.*

1. A. In a cinema. B. In a restaurant.
   C. In a drugstore. D. In a factory.
2. A. 7：45. B. 7：30.
   C. 8：00. D. 7：15.
3. A. On the second floor. B. In a women's department.
   C. In a shopping center. D. At a men's store.
4. A. In the library. B. In the teaching building.
   C. On the grass. D. On the bicycle.
5. A. Read the newspaper. B. Go jogging.
   C. Rest all day. D. Watch TV.
6. A. She will go to a concert this weekend.
   B. She will go to a concert with her boyfriend.

C. She won't go to a concert this weekend.

D. She won't go to a concert with her sister.

7. A. At 10: 00 a. m. . B. At 10: 30 p. m. .

C. At 11 p. m. . D. At 7 p. m. .

8. A. A success. B. A trouble.

C. A failure. D. we don't know.

9. A. The man's cousin. B. The man's aunt.

C. The man's uncle. D. The man's daughter.

10. A. The price of a pair of trousers. B. The price of a pair of glasses.

C. The price of a pair of gloves. D. The price of a pair of shoes.

Section B (2 × 10)

Directions: In this section you will hear 2 short talks. Each talk will be spoken twice. After the talk you will be asked questions. When you hear a question, read the four possible answers in your test paper and choose the best one to the question you have heard. Then, mark your answer by blackening the corresponding letter of your choice on the Answer Sheet.

Questions 11 – 15 are based on the passage you have just heard.

11. A. Thanksgiving Day. B. Christmas Day.

C. Black Friday. D. New Year's Day.

12. A. Traveling. B. Shopping.

C. Eating. D. Sightseeing.

13. A. Thanksgiving Day. B. Christmas Day.

C. Black Friday. D. Holiday.

14. A. 6,000 pounds. B. 1,600 pounds.

C. 3,600 pounds. D. 6,600 pounds.

15. A. 8 hours. B. 10 hours.

C. 14 hours. D. 18 hours.

Questions 16 – 20 are based on the passage you have just heard.

16. A. The Mediterranean Sea and the Red Sea.

B. Egypt and French.

C. North and East of Egypt.

D. Egypt and Israel.

17. A. In 1859. B. In 1869. C. In 1956. D. In 1957.

18. A. About 20 kilometers. B. About 30 kilometers.

C. About 300 kilometers. D. About 200 kilometers.

19. A. An Italian engineer.
B. A British engineer.
C. A French engineer.
D. An American engineer.

20. A. The ships of all nations can use the canal in peacetime and wartime.
B. The Suez Canal can only be used by the Egyptians.
C. The ships of all nations can use the canal in peacetime.
D. The ships of all nations can use the canal as long as they get the permission of the United Nations.

Part II Reading Comprehension (40 points)

Directions: There are 4 passages in this part. Each passage is followed by some questions or unfinished statements. For each of them there are 4 choices marked A, B, C and D. You should decide on the best choice and mark your answer by blackening the corresponding letter on the Answer Sheet.

Questions 21 – 25 are based on the following passage:

Climate change talks ended Friday in Lima, Peru. The international negotiations included more than 10,000 participants from about 200 countries. Participants aimed to create a plan for reducing greenhouse gases around the world. They expected the plan to develop into a firm agreement at the next major climate change talks in Paris next year. The participants—including the Secretary-General of the United Nations, Ban Ki-moon—agreed on the importance of limiting climate change. But they could not always agree on how to reach their goal. Representatives from developing nations repeated their belief that wealthy countries should take more responsibility for reducing their carbon pollution. But U. S. Secretary of State John Kerry said Thursday that more than half of global warming gases come from developing nations. He said those nations must also make changes. Scientists warn that greenhouse gases are causing the world's temperature to rise. Global warming, they say, will cause droughts, floods and rising oceans.

21. What was the purpose of climate change talks held in Lima, Peru?
A. It aimed to hold international negotiations.
B. It aimed to make a plan for reducing warming gases throughout the world.
C. It aimed to reach an agreement on how to limit climate change.
D. It aimed to reduce greenhouse gases from developing countries.

22. What was the aim of the next climate change talks held in Paris?
A. It aimed to make the plan become into realities.
B. It aimed to make an agreement on the importance of limiting climate change.
C. It aimed to promote developing countries take more responsibilities.

D. It aimed to make the plan develop into an agreement.

23. What did the participants achieve in climate change talks in Lima, Peru?

A. They achieved nothing.

B. They stressed the importance of limiting climate change.

C. They found a way to reach their goal of limiting climate change.

D. They agreed on the importance of limiting climate change.

24. What was the opinion of representatives from developing nations?

A. They thought that it was none of their business.

B. They thought that both developing nations and developed nations should work together to limit climate change.

C. They believed that developed nations should undertake more responsibility for limiting climate change.

D. They believed that they should take more responsibility for limiting climate change.

25. According to scientists, what will global warming cause?

A. Global warming will cause droughts.

B. Global warming will cause carbon pollution.

C. Global warming will lead to droughts, floods and cancer.

D. Global warming will lead to droughts, floods and ocean rising.

Questions 26 – 30 are based on the following passage:

Do you re-use plastic bags? If you don't, you're not alone. And so to reduce waste and protect the environment, the UK authorities have decided to hit shoppers where it hurts the most: their pockets! A required carrier bag charge has been introduced in Scotland. Shoppers who want a new bag will have to pay a minimum of 5 pounds. The Scottish government has estimated that 800 million single-use bags are given out by supermarkets every year. And where do they go? Environment Secretary Richard Lochhead says: "Huge numbers of these bags end up as litter, clogging up our seas and natural habitats, affecting many sorts of wildlife and marine species in particular." Mr Lochhead wants people to stop and think about whether they really need another bag. He says: "Alternatives like bags-for-life are easy to get and are much more sustainable." The charge isn't a tax so the money collected doesn't go into the public coffers. Some retailers have said they'll donate it to good causes — some of them to preserve the environment. Scotland is the third part of the UK to introduce the charge. Wales did it in 2011 and bag use there has since fallen by 79%. In Northern Ireland the drop was 72% after they introduced the charge there last year. In 2015, it will be England's turn to ask shoppers to pay for their bags. Only smaller retailers will be exempt. Many people are used to carrying an old plastic bag with them when they go out, just in case they decide to buy something. What about you: do you think paying for plastic bags is a good idea?

26. What is the passage mainly about?

A. Re-use plastic bags. B. Recycling plastic bags.

C. Environmental Protection. D. Pay for your bag.

27. Which of the following is true?

A. Scottish government gives out free bags.

B. Scotland has charged for carrier bags.

C. People in Scotland are willing to pay for carrier bags.

D. People in Scotland have to pay 5 pounds for a bag.

28. According to the passage, what are the disadvantages of single-use bags?

A. They end up as litter.

B. They clog up our seas and natural habitats.

C. They affect many kinds of wildlife and marine species.

D. All of the above.

29. What does the underlined word (Line 2) mean in this passage?

A. Preserve. B. Prevent. C. Reserve. D. Promise.

30. We can infer from this passage that ______ hasn't introduced the charge.

A. Scotland B. Northern Ireland

C. England D. the United Kingdom

Questions 31 – 35 are based on the following passage:

Most children have heard their parents at one time or another yell "sit up straight!" or "don't slouch!" In the past, this was usually heard at the dinner table as children ate dinner. But these days, it is also heard around another activity—video games.

Ten – year old Owaish Batliwala, from Mumbai, India, admits he spends three to four hours each day playing games on his tablet computer. His mother Mehzabin became concerned when her son started saying that his neck hurt.

Sadia Vanjara is a physical therapist. She says the number of young children with chronic pain in their necks, arms and shoulders is on the rise. Dr. Vanjara says the pain is not from aging, accidents or disease. It is from poor posture, or body position, while playing video games.

This is a problem in many parts of the world. But there are more smartphone users in India than anywhere else in the world, except China. Networking equipment company Cisco estimates that the number of smartphone users in India will increase from 140 million today to 651 million by 2020. 19 – year old student Nida Jameel says she feels pain in the finger which holds the weight of her smartphone most of the day. She says she uses her smartphone 24/7. This means 24 hours a day, seven days a week, or all the time.

Doctors say that holding your smartphone in a bad position could lead to problems with your hands and fingers. Correct posture can help prevent pain. Dr. Vanjara teaches children how to hold their gadgets correctly. She tells a patient to hold the gadget in front of the face. She says that bending the head down to look at the device, strains the neck and creates an unhealthy bend to the back.

Sadia Vanjara predicts we will see not only physical but psychological and emotional problems resulting from overuse of gadgets.

Experts advise taking breaks from using a computer or other device often. Stand up. Stretch your legs, back, shoulders and arms. And when your work or school work is done, unplug and exercise.

31. Which is the best title of the passage?

A. Overuse of gadgets can cause physical and psychological problems.

B. The number of young children with pain in their necks and fingers is rising.

C. Correct posture can help prevent pain.

D. Too much gaming is a pain in the neck.

32. ________ made Owaish Batliwala's neck hurt.

A. A car accident. B. A rare disease.

C. A fall from the horse. D. Overuse of the computer.

33. ________ has the most smartphone users in the world.

A. Canada B. America C. China D. India

34. What does the underlined word "posture" (Para. 3) mean?

A. Distance. B. Body. C. Health. D. Position.

35. According to the passage, the following suggestions EXCEPT ________ can prevent pain.

A. Have more healthy food.

B. Have a rest very often when using computers.

C. Do daily exercise.

D. Unplug when your school work is done.

Questions 36 – 40 are based on the following passage:

Many students say there is no easy way to write college papers. This may be especially true if English is not your first language. Most teachers agree that there is no single "correct" way to create a personal essay or a research paper. But there are methods to help you structure your papers.

One way often used to structure writing is the traditional five-paragraph essay. Many students learn this form in middle and high school. The paragraphs follow conventions, or established rules. The first paragraph is introductory. It tells the reader what the paper is about.

It is followed by three paragraphs containing evidence that support the writer's argument. The final paragraph is the conclusion. It provides a reasoned opinion based on the evidence.

Allison Cummings teaches English at Southern New Hampshire University. She is among many professors who find this form too simple for college work. Still, on the positive side, Ms. Cummings says the five-paragraph essay form teaches a student some tools for writing a paper. She says the form teaches the need for the opening statement, or thesis. This thesis tells the reader what will come next. In addition, students who have learned to write a five-paragraph essay know they must provide evidence. And Ms. Cummings says the writer will know a conclusion is required. But she also says the five-paragraph essay falls far short of college writing needs.

So, if a traditional method for structuring a research paper does not work, what steps can help you structure your writing? Ms. Cummings says doing research for a paper helps some students in their writing. The teacher says noting the way the research is structured can help students organize their own writing. She offers sample outlines-examples for organizing papers, and she also provides her students with examples of successful and unsuccessful student papers. That way, her class can see what works in a piece of writing and what does not.

36. Which is the best title of the passage?
    A. Expand Your Skills for Writing College Papers
    B. There Is No Easy Way to Write College Papers
    C. Five-paragraph Essay
    D. Some Tools for Writing a Paper

37. ________ is the traditional way of writing a paper?
    A. Following conventions or established rules
    B. The five-paragraph essay form
    C. Sample Outline
    D. Examples of Student Papers
38. What is the disadvantage of traditional way of writing a paper?
    A. It is too complicated for the students to follow.
    B. It is difficult for the students to provide evidence.
    C. It is too simple to meet college writing needs.
    D. The traditional method for structuring a paper does not work.
39. How many ways of writing a paper are mentioned in the passage?
    A. One. B. Two. C. Three. D. Four.
40. What does the underlined word mean in the last paragraph?
    A. Structures. B. Writings. C. Methods. D. Papers.

Part III. Choose the best answer (20 points)

Directions: There are 20 incomplete sentences in this part. For each sentence there are 4 choices marked A, B, C and D. Choose the ONE answer that best completes the sentence. Then mark your answer by blackening the corresponding letter on the Answer Sheet.

41. This is not the first time the world ________ Ebola.
    A. has heard　B. has listened to　C. has heard of　D. has heard from
42. By the time we reach our 50s and 60s we may have trouble remembering simple things ________ the names of new people we meet or where we put our car keys.
    A. such as　B. for example　C. for instance　D. such like
43. The man who ________ the program is my brother, and he spent a few days creating the game.
    A. developed　B. collected　C. played　D. watched
44. Over the years, ________ of singers and musicians have recorded "White Christmas". But the version most people still know best was sung by Bing Crosby.
    A. two hundred　B. hundreds　C. many　D. a few
45. Six people escaped from the restaurant just before the police raided it. The dead include two men and one woman. Four other people ________.
    A. damaged　B. harmed　C. were destroyed　D. were injured
46. I know he hasn't finished the work but, ________, he's very busy.
    A. above all　B. in case　C. because of　D. after all
47. It is said that in Africa more than a third of the population has no ________ to the health care and advanced education.
    A. control　B. opportunity　C. access　D. success
48. Graduates ______ many job offers, and they were able to get jobs with high salaries and benefits such as insurance and paid vacations.
    A. accepted　B. adapted　C. adopted　D. received
49. They are waiting ________ to see who will succeed him.
    A. anxiously　B. weakly　C. disappointingly　D. friendly
50. The ice was not thick enough to ________ the weight of marching men.
    A. bear　B. catch　C. lift　D. support
51. Why not try another way ________ you may do your experiment better and more quickly?
    A. for which　B. that　C. with which　D. in that
52. Hong Kong is such a dynamic city that we decide to stay for ________ two weeks.
    A. the other　B. another　C. the others　D. others
53. Tom as well as his friends ________ to music.
    A. like to listen　B. likes to listen　C. like to hear　D. likes to hear

54. I don't believe what you said. It ________ be true.
    A. mustn't   B. can't   C. shouldn't   D. needn't
55. Cooking needs ________ patience and time, but it is ________ enjoyable experience.
    A. a; the   B. / ; /   C. the; an   D. / ; an
56. He ________ hardly ________ the station when the train ________.
    A. had; entered; had left   B. / ; entered; left
    C. have; entered; left   D. had; entered; left
57. She talked about London as though she ________ there.
    A. had been   B. had gone   C. went   D. was
58. So little ________ with each other that the neighboring countries could not settle their difference.
    A. they agreed   B. agreed they   C. did they agree   D. they did agree
59. ________ John and Lily who taught us how to make cakes.
    A. It was   B. Who were   C. It were   D. There were
60. Many men still have difficulty ________ a woman as a business partner.
    A. accept   B. to accept   C. receiving   D. accepting

Part IV. Cloze (20 points)

Directions: There are 20 blanks in the following passage. For each blank there are 4 choices marked A, B, C and D. Choose the ONE answer that best fits into the passage. Then mark your answer by blackening the corresponding letter on the Answer Sheet.

Nothing succeeds without confidence. When you are truly and __61__ confident, it radiates from you like sunlight, and attracts __62__ to you like a magnet. It's important to believe in __63__. Believe that you can do it __64__ any circumstances, __65__ you believe you can, then you really will. The belief keeps you __66__ answers, which means that __67__ soon you will get them. Confidence is __68__ an attitude. It comes from knowing exactly __69__ you are going and exactly __70__ you are going to get there. It comes __71__ acting with integrity and confidence. It comes from a strong sense of __72__. It comes from a strong commitment __73__ responsibility, rather than just letting life __74__. One way to develop self – confidence is to do the thing you __75__ and to get a record of successful experiences behind you. Confidence is __76__ and understanding. It is not arrogant. Arrogance is born out of fear and insecurity, __77__ confidence comes from strength and integrity. Confidence means that you know you are capable of accomplishing __78__ you want. If your life is not what you want it to be, you have the power to change __79__. Live with your goals and your plan of action. Live __80__ moment with your priorities in mind. Act with your own purpose, and you will have the life you want.

61. A. hardly	B. justifiably	C. only	D. justly
62. A. reward	B. prize	C. success	D. successor
63. A. yourself	B. it	C. him	D. you
64. A. with	B. on	C. for	D. under
65. A. because	B. even if	C. because if	D. if
66. A. searching for	B. search for	C. in search	D. searching
67. A. so	B. pretty	C. as	D. how
68. A. more than	B. less than	C. no less than	D. no more than
69. A. which	B. what	C. where	D. whose
70. A. which	B. what	C. that	D. how
71. A. from	B. to	C. over	D. out
72. A. purpose	B. humor	C. smell	D. security
73. A. took	B. take	C. taking	D. to take
74. A. happens	B. happen	C. happening	D. to happen
75. A. afraid	B. fear	C. worry	D. scary
76. A. compass	B. passion	C. compassionate	D. passionate
77. A. when	B. however	C. and	D. while
78. A. that	B. nothing	C. something	D. anything
79. A. it	B. them	C. that	D. this
80. A. either	B. each	C. neither	D. all

Paper Ⅱ (40 points)

Part V. Proof Reading (10 points)

Directions: Read carefully each line to find out the mistakes.

1. *If there is no mistake in the line, mark "√" on the right hand side.*
2. *If there is a redundant (多余的) word in the line, first write it off with a slanting line (\), and then write the word on the right hand side with the slanting line.*
3. *If there is a word missing in the line, put a missing word sign (∧) there and write the missing word on the right hand side.*
4. *If there is a wrong word in the line, draw a line under it and write the correct one on the right hand side.*

Example:

When I have free time I go ∧ a long walk. Some　　(1) for

people read \the books or watch television while　　(2) \the

others have sports. Charles and Linda Mason do all (3) √
of these things as well as climbed buildings. (4) climbing; climb

The best way to maintain a health vitamin and 81. ______
mineral intake is a good diet. There is not necessary 82. ______
or advise to go out and buy some vitamin supplements 83. ______
in order to achieve your suggesting nutritional levels. Many 84. ______
over – the – counter vitamin are chemically processed 85. ______
and are completely absorbed into the system. It is 86. ______
also easy to take too many vitamins, particular 87. ______
when taking supplements of some vitamins and 88. ______
minerals, which will do harm to you. The likelihood
of doing this that is far little with food; therefore it is always 89. ______
best to obtain most of your vitamin and mineral
requirements to unprocessed foods. 90. ______

Part VI. Fill in the blanks (10 points)

Directions: There are 10 blanks in the following passage and 12 words in the following box. You are required to select 10 of the given words to complete the passage. Pay attention to the correct form of the words. Each word can be used only once.

transform	impressive	besides	travel	re-shape	volunteer
transfer	global	except	organize	follow	relax

Many of us love to __91__ abroad and __92__ ourselves during the journey. Perhaps not everyone originally realized how much we would learn from our __93__ adventures. And how insights gained would __94__ into re-defining our lives, __95__ them in surprisingly new ways. During last three years, __96__ Singapore and those south-east Asia counties like Malaysia and Thailand, I've also visited, which also happened to be the most __97__ places, England for a business trip __98__ by school where my team tried to set up a Chinese language school in London. In the North-west of US I joined work and travel program to work at a snow mountain near Seattle, then I had a small trip to India, __99__ by a long journey to Chile, then I __100__ to be a farmer at an eco-farm in the center of a forest, then I travelled to many other places at south America.

Part VII. Composition (20 points)

Directions: *Write a composition of about* 150 *words according to the given points.*

假定你是暨南大学的学生李华。一批来自澳洲的大学生即将访问你校并参加一系列的文化交流活动。请根据以下提示，给澳洲的活动承办方写封邮件，告知活动详情：①表示对客人的欢迎；②介绍与本地相关的信息（如天气、饮食等）；③介绍活动安排：学习中国书法和武术等课程，参观当地的企业，广州文化游（珠江夜游、电视塔等）；④表达对客人的祝愿。

文化交流活动：culture exchange program
书法：Chinese calligraphy
武术：Chinese martial arts
广州文化游：Guangzhou cultural tour
珠江夜游：Pearl River Night Cruise
电视塔：TV Tower

暨南大学、华侨大学联合招收港澳地区、台湾省、华侨、华人及其他外籍学生入学考试样题

英 语

答题卡

选择题区

1 [A] [B] [C] [D]	6 [A] [B] [C] [D]	11 [A] [B] [C] [D]	16 [A] [B] [C] [D]
2 [A] [B] [C] [D]	7 [A] [B] [C] [D]	12 [A] [B] [C] [D]	17 [A] [B] [C] [D]
3 [A] [B] [C] [D]	8 [A] [B] [C] [D]	13 [A] [B] [C] [D]	18 [A] [B] [C] [D]
4 [A] [B] [C] [D]	9 [A] [B] [C] [D]	14 [A] [B] [C] [D]	19 [A] [B] [C] [D]
5 [A] [B] [C] [D]	10 [A] [B] [C] [D]	15 [A] [B] [C] [D]	20 [A] [B] [C] [D]
21 [A] [B] [C] [D]	26 [A] [B] [C] [D]	31 [A] [B] [C] [D]	36 [A] [B] [C] [D]
22 [A] [B] [C] [D]	27 [A] [B] [C] [D]	32 [A] [B] [C] [D]	37 [A] [B] [C] [D]
23 [A] [B] [C] [D]	28 [A] [B] [C] [D]	33 [A] [B] [C] [D]	38 [A] [B] [C] [D]
24 [A] [B] [C] [D]	29 [A] [B] [C] [D]	34 [A] [B] [C] [D]	39 [A] [B] [C] [D]
25 [A] [B] [C] [D]	30 [A] [B] [C] [D]	35 [A] [B] [C] [D]	40 [A] [B] [C] [D]
41 [A] [B] [C] [D]	46 [A] [B] [C] [D]	51 [A] [B] [C] [D]	56 [A] [B] [C] [D]
42 [A] [B] [C] [D]	47 [A] [B] [C] [D]	52 [A] [B] [C] [D]	57 [A] [B] [C] [D]
43 [A] [B] [C] [D]	48 [A] [B] [C] [D]	53 [A] [B] [C] [D]	58 [A] [B] [C] [D]
44 [A] [B] [C] [D]	49 [A] [B] [C] [D]	54 [A] [B] [C] [D]	59 [A] [B] [C] [D]
45 [A] [B] [C] [D]	50 [A] [B] [C] [D]	55 [A] [B] [C] [D]	60 [A] [B] [C] [D]
61 [A] [B] [C] [D]	66 [A] [B] [C] [D]	71 [A] [B] [C] [D]	76 [A] [B] [C] [D]
62 [A] [B] [C] [D]	67 [A] [B] [C] [D]	72 [A] [B] [C] [D]	77 [A] [B] [C] [D]
63 [A] [B] [C] [D]	68 [A] [B] [C] [D]	73 [A] [B] [C] [D]	78 [A] [B] [C] [D]
64 [A] [B] [C] [D]	69 [A] [B] [C] [D]	74 [A] [B] [C] [D]	79 [A] [B] [C] [D]
65 [A] [B] [C] [D]	70 [A] [B] [C] [D]	75 [A] [B] [C] [D]	80 [A] [B] [C] [D]

以下为非选择题答题区，必须用黑色字迹的钢笔或签字笔在指定的黑色框区域内作答，否则答案无效。

Part V. Proof Reading（10 points）

81. ________ 82. ________ 83. ________ 84. ________ 85. ________

86. ________ 87. ________ 88. ________ 89. ________ 90. ________

Part VI. Fill in the blanks (10 points)

91. ________ 92. ________ 93. ________ 94. ________ 95. ________

96. ________ 97. ________ 98. ________ 99. ________ 100. ________

Part VII. Composition (20 points)

Script & Key

Part I. Listening Comprehension (30 points)

Section A

1. M: Hello. What can I do for you?
   W: Could you fill this prescription for me, please.
   M: I'll take care of it right away.
   W: And I'd like something for sunburn.
   M: You might try this. It's a new product.
   Q: Where are the two speakers?
2. W: Where have you been? It's 7: 45 now, and the film started a quarter ago.
   M: I' m sorry, I got lost.
   Q: When did the film begin?
3. W: I'd like to buy a new dress.
   M: The women's department is on the second floor, Madam.
   Q: Where does the conversation take place?
4. W: Where did you say you found your key to the bicycle?
   M: It was lying on the grass between the library and the teaching building.
   Q: Where did the man find the key?
5. W: What do you usually do on Saturdays?
   M: I go jogging in the morning, read newspapers in the afternoon and watch TV in the evening. I don't like to rest all day and do nothing.
   Q: What does the man usually do on Saturday evening?
6. M: Well, do you have anything planned for the Saturday?
   W: Eh, I'm kind of busy. Why do you ask?
   M: I was wondering if we could go to a concert together.
   W: I'd love to, but I'm really busy this weekend.
   Q: What does the woman mean?
7. M: Excuse me, what time does the swimming pool close in the evening?
   W: It all depends. We close at 10: 30 p. m. on weekdays, at 11 p. m. at weekends.
   M: Thanks a lot.
   W: You are welcome.
   Q: When does the swimming pool close on Sundays?
8. W: Charlie, do you think you will get the job this time?
   M: Quite hopeful. I answered the woman interviewer's questions quite successfully.
   W: Did she ask you whether you would like to work under a woman manager?
   M: Yes, she did, and my answer was a loud YES.

Q: What does the man think of his job interview?

9. M: My uncle is angry with his daughter.

W: Really? What has his daughter done?

M: She has broken her cup again.

Q: Who has broken the cup again?

10. M: How much are these shoes?

W: They are $ 425.

M: With the same money I can buy a pair of trousers and a pair of gloves.

W: But this is the best price in town.

Q: What is the man talking about with the woman?

Section B

Black Friday is the day after Thanksgiving. This year it falls on November 28th. As Thanksgiving Day revolves around the eating, so Black Friday revolves around the shopping. It has become the biggest day of the year for American retailers as they discount thousands of products, kick – starting the Christmas shopping season. According to one story the name thus refers to shops doing such booming trade that they go from the red into the black. It might equally be named because of the casualty rate. Shoppers get hurt in the stampede for bargains. Some have even died.

Since they do not celebrate Thanksgiving, Brits had never taken to Black Friday, until last year. Then, some British retailers joined American – owned companies like Amazon to introduce big savings. This year many more have embraced it. Visa Europe predicts that shoppers will spend 6,000 per second on the day. John Lewis, a big London department store, is opening for its longest day ever, from 8 a. m. to 10 p. m..

11. What is the passage talk about?
12. According to the passage, what is Thanksgiving Day about?
13. What is the biggest day of the year for American retailers?
14. According to Visa Europe, how much will shoppers spend per second on the day?
15. How long will John Lewis open on the day?

What do you know about the Suez Canal? Today I will share my lecture on the Suez Canal with you. I hope you will like it.

In 1869, a new waterway was completed. This new waterway connects the Mediterranean Sea and the Gulf of Suez which is part of the Red Sea. This canal, which lies in a desert area in northeastern Egypt, is called the Suez Canal.

The Suez Canal runs from about two hundred kilometers from the port of Suez, on the Gulf of Suez, to Port Said, on the Mediterranean Sea. Some parts of the canal are very narrow. So two ships cannot pass there at the same time. One ship must wait in a certain place or in one of the lakes until the canal is passable again.

A French engineer Ferdinard de Lesseps, was the man who was in charge of the building of the Suez Canal. Work began in 1859 and continued until 1869. In honour of the completion of the Suez Canal, a famous Italian musician named Giuseppe Verdi wrote an opera, "Aida", which is one of the most famous operas ever written.

There was an international agreement that states the ships of all nations could use the canal in peacetime and wartime. However, this has not always been possible. For example, in 1956, there was a war among the French, British, Egyptians and Israelis. The canal was reopened in 1957 with the help of the United Nations.

16. Which two places does the Suez Canal connect?
17. When was the Suez Canal completed?
18. How long does the Suez Canal run from the port of Suez to Port Said?
19. Who was in charge of the building of the Suez Canal?
20. What was the international agreement about the Suez Canal?

Key to the Sample Test

Paper I (110 points)

Part I Listening Comprehension (30 points)

Section A (1 × 10)

1. C 2. B 3. C 4. C 5. D 6. C 7. C 8. A 9. A 10. D

Section B (2 × 10)

11. C 12. C 13. C 14. A 15. C 16. A 17. B 18. D 19. C 20. A

Part II. Reading Comprehension (40 points)

21. B 22. D 23. D 24. C 25. D 26. D 27. B 28. D 29. A 30. C
31. D 32. D 33. C 34. D 35. A 36. A 37. B 38. C 39. B 40. C

Part III. Choose the best answer (20 points)

41. C 42. A 43. A 44. B 45. D 46. D 47. C 48. D 49. A 50. A
51. B 52. B 53. B 54. B 55. D 56. D 57. A 58. C 59. A 60. D

Part IV. Cloze (20 points)

61. B 62. C 63. A 64. D 65. C 66. A 67. B 68. A 69. C 70. D
71. A 72. A 73. D 74. B 75. B 76. C 77. D 78. D 79. A 80. B

Paper II (40 points)

Part V. Proof Reading (10 points)

81. health— healthy
82. There — It
83. advise — advisable
84. suggesting — suggested
85. vitamin — vitamins
86. are ∧ not
87. particular — particularly
88. √
89. that
90. to — from

Part VI. Fill in the blanks (10 points)

91. travel 92. relax 93. global 94. transform 95. re-shaping
96. besides 97. impressive 98. organized 99. followed 100. volunteered

Part VII. Composition (20 points)

Omitted.

历 史

考试要求

（1）历史科考试内容包括中国历史和世界近现代史两部分。本学科要求考生掌握最重要的历史事实；通过历史基础知识的学习，理解历史事件的由来、发展及其相互关系。
（2）整理、分析、综合及评价史实，运用历史资料及有关论述，得出适当结论。
（3）初步掌握探究历史的方法，能独立思考，能较深入地探究重大历史问题。

考试范围与内容

中国古代史

一、引言

中国历史的发端及分期

二、秦、汉

1. 秦的统一　秦朝的中央集权制
2. 刘邦建汉与休养生息　文景之治　汉武帝的统治

三、隋、唐

1. 隋朝的统一　隋初的政治经济改革
2. 唐朝的建立　唐朝的政治经济制度　唐太宗　武则天　唐玄宗
安史之乱与唐朝的衰落

四、宋、元

1. 北宋加强中央集权
2. 元朝的建立　巩固统一的措施

五、明、清（鸦片战争以前）

1. 明朝的建立　君主专制的加强　明朝灭亡　清军入关

2. 清朝加强中央集权的措施　康乾盛世　反对分裂、巩固统一、抗击外来侵略的重大斗争　清朝的疆域

中国近代史

一、鸦片战争

1. 林则徐与禁烟运动
2. 鸦片战争的经过
3. 战争的影响
   中英《南京条约》及其附件
   新思想的萌发
4. 第二次鸦片战争的爆发
   《天津条约》　《北京条约》　沙俄侵占中国大片领土

二、太平天国

1. 太平天国运动的兴起和发展
   金田起义　定都天京　《天朝田亩制度》
2. 太平天国后期的斗争
   天京变乱　《资政新篇》　太平天国运动的失败及历史意义

三、中国资本主义的产生和资本主义国家侵略中国的加剧

1. 洋务运动
   总理衙门　洋务派　洋务运动的成果及其破产的原因
2. 中国资本主义的产生
3. 甲午中日战争
   边疆危机　战争的爆发　平壤保卫战　黄海大战　辽东半岛之战　威海卫之战　《马关条约》
4. 瓜分中国的狂潮
   列强对中国的资本输出　强占"租借地"和划分"势力范围"
   美国的"门户开放"政策
5. 八国联军侵华战争
   义和团的兴起　八国联军侵华战争　《辛丑条约》

四、戊戌变法

康有为和梁启超的变法活动　百日维新和戊戌政变
戊戌变法的历史意义及其失败原因

五、辛亥革命和清朝的灭亡

1. 资产阶级革命运动的兴起

孙中山和兴中会的建立　民主革命思想的传播和资产阶级革命团体的建立　中国同盟会的成立及其政治纲领

2. 资产阶级革命运动的发展和辛亥革命的爆发

广州黄花岗起义　四川保路运动　武昌起义

3. 中华民国的成立

《中华民国临时约法》　辛亥革命的功绩和教训

六、北洋军阀的统治

1. 反对袁世凯统治的斗争

"二次革命"与护国运动

2. 段祺瑞的独裁统治和护法运动

张勋复辟　护法运动

七、五四运动和中国共产党的成立

1. 新文化运动

新文化运动的兴起　新文化运动的内容

2. 五四运动

五四运动的背景、经过与历史意义

3. 中国共产党的诞生

中共"一大"、"二大"

八、国民革命运动

1. 第一次国共合作

中国共产党制定革命统一战线政策　中国国民党第一次全国代表大会　黄埔陆军军官学校

2. 国民革命运动的兴起

北京政变和孙中山北上　五卅运动　省港大罢工　北伐战争

3. 国共关系破裂和南京国民政府的成立

蒋介石与汪精卫的反革命政变　南京国民政府　东北易帜

九、第二次国共合作与抗日战争

1. 国共内战　"九一八"事变和"一·二八"事变　"一二·九"运动　西安事变

2. 抗日战争

抗日战争的三个阶段　卢沟桥事变　"八一三"事变与南京大屠杀

抗日民族统一战线　八路军和新四军　国民党正面战场的四大会战　百团大战
抗日战争的胜利

十、解放战争与中华人民共和国的建立

重庆谈判与《双十协定》　内战爆发　三大战役　渡江战役　大陆的解放
中国人民政治协商会议与中华人民共和国的建立

中国现代史

一、中华人民共和国建立初期的经济政治

经济建设在曲折中发展　“文革”动乱

二、改革开放和祖国的统一大业

改革开放及其成就　外交领域的主要成就　香港和澳门的回归
反对“台独”和争取和平统一的斗争

世界历史

一、引言

世界历史概述

二、英国资产阶级革命

1. 英国资本主义的发展
2. 王权和议会的斗争
3. 克伦威尔的独裁统治
4. 君主立宪制的确立

1688 年政变　《权利法案》

三、美国独立战争

波士顿倾茶事件　莱克星顿枪声　乔治·华盛顿　《独立宣言》
美国联邦政府的成立　1787 年宪法

四、法国大革命和法兰西第一帝国

启蒙运动　攻克巴士底狱　《人权宣言》　1792 年 8 月起义
瓦尔密大捷　法兰西第一共和国的成立　吉伦特派的统治和雅各宾派的统治
雾月政变　法兰西第一帝国和维也纳体系

五、第一次工业革命与19世纪六七十年代资产阶级革命和改良

1. 英国工业革命
   工业革命的前提和条件　发明与创造　工业革命的后果
2. 沙皇俄国的改革和侵略扩张
   彼得一世改革　1861年农奴制改革　俄国的侵略扩张
3. 德国和意大利的统一
4. 日本明治维新
   幕府统治的危机　武装倒幕　明治维新
5. 美国南北战争
   林肯与废奴主义　内战爆发　《宅地法》和《解放黑人奴隶宣言》
   美国内战的历史意义

六、第二次工业革命

第二次工业革命的主要成就　工业革命对社会的影响

七、第一次世界大战

1. 三国同盟和三国协约
2. 萨拉热窝事件与大战爆发
3. 重要战役
4. 大战结束

八、俄国十月社会主义革命

1. 1917年的二月革命与十月革命
2. 苏联的建立

九、两次大战期间的国际关系与国际危机

1. 凡尔赛—华盛顿体系
   巴黎和会　《凡尔赛和约》　国际联盟　华盛顿会议
2. 1929—1933年资本主义世界的经济危机
3. 罗斯福新政
4. 德国和日本的法西斯化

十、第二次世界大战

1. 慕尼黑阴谋
2. 大战的进程
   德国突袭波兰　法国的溃败　德国突袭苏联　太平洋战争爆发
   世界反法西斯同盟的形成　斯大林格勒战役　中途岛战役

3．世界反法西斯战争的伟大胜利

意大利投降　德黑兰会议　《开罗宣言》　诺曼底登陆　雅尔塔会议　德国投降　波茨坦会议　日本投降

4．世界反法西斯战争胜利的伟大历史意义

十一、战后世界

1．雅尔塔体系

2．冷战

3．世界格局的新变化

考试形式

考试采用闭卷、书面笔答的形式，考试时间为120分钟，试卷满分为150分（选择题80分，非选择题70分）。

试卷结构与题型

（1）非选择题中材料解析题占20分，中国史、世界史各一题，其中中国史部分的材料为较浅显的文言文或现代文。

（2）非选择题中问答题占30分，中国古代史、中国近现代史、世界近代史和世界现代史各一题，可任选其中两题作答。

（3）非选择题中的论述题占20分，共两题，中国史和世界史各一题，可任选其中一题作答。该题不预设固定答案，考生可以发挥个人见解。

考生复习参考资料

1．唐景阳. 暨南大学、华侨大学联合招收港澳地区、台湾省、华侨、华人及其他外籍学生入学考试复习丛书·历史. 广州：暨南大学出版社，2015.

2．唐景阳. 暨南大学、华侨大学及全国联招考试模拟试题丛书·历史. 广州：暨南大学出版社，2013.

3．唐景阳. 暨南大学、华侨大学两校联招及全国联招2004—2011年试题详解丛书·历史. 广州：暨南大学出版社，2013.

样卷

暨南大学、华侨大学联合招收港澳地区、台湾省、华侨、华人及其他外籍学生入学考试样题

科目：历　史

答卷时间：120 分钟

一、选择题（本大题共 20 小题，每小题 4 分，共 80 分。在每小题列出的四个选项中，只有一项是符合题目要求的，请将答题卡中相应的字母代号涂黑）

1. 下列哪一项不是秦统一全国后采取的统一措施？

　A. 统一驰道长度　　B. 统一车轨宽度

　C. 统一重量　　D. 统一文字

2. 下列说法中，正确的是

　A. 秦朝末年，刘邦和项羽争夺天下，历史上称“楚汉之争”

　B. 西汉建国之初，采用儒家之术，实行“休养生息”政策

　C. 汉惠帝时，“萧规曹随”，继续推行“休养生息”政策。这里“萧规曹随”中的“萧”是指丞相萧何，“曹”是指丞相曹操

　D. “休养生息”政策推行了六七十年，到汉武帝时，西汉经济的发展达到鼎盛

3. 隋唐的三省六部制中，中书省的职责是

　A. 管理官吏　　B. 草拟政令　　C. 监察百官　　D. 执行政令

4. 北宋加强中央集权的措施最大的弊端是导致北宋中后期出现以下哪一现象？

　A. 冗官　　B. 冗兵　　C. 冗费　　D. 积贫积弱

5. 下列哪一项属于乾隆帝的政绩？

　A. 废除人头税，实行“摊丁入亩”　　B. 雅克萨自卫战

　C. 平定回部叛乱　　D. 平定三藩之乱

6. 下列哪一项不是中英《南京条约》的内容？

　A. 割让香港岛给英国

　B. 赔款军费 2 100 万银圆

　C. 开放广州、厦门、福州、宁波、上海五处为通商口岸

　D. 废除“公行”制度

7. 近代侵略中国并火烧圆明园的是

　A. 英国军队　　B. 英法联军　　C. 八国联军　　D. 日本军队

8. 下列关于太平天国《天朝田亩制度》的说法正确的是

　A. 定都天京后颁发

　B. 只在太平天国占领区域实施

C. 没有反映广大农民的迫切愿望，故而成为一纸空文
D. 反映了先进中国人的愿望

9. 下列属于洋务运动期间洋务派创办的民用工业的是
A. 安庆军械所 B. 福州船政局 C. 轮船招商局 D. 发昌机器厂

10. 1894 年中日黄海大战中，率“经远号”与敌激战并壮烈牺牲的清军将领是
A. 丁汝昌 B. 刘步蟾 C. 林永升 D. 邓世昌

11. 20 世纪初，最早提出推翻清政府，建立一个独立、民主、自由的“中华共和国”的革命宣传家是
A. 章炳麟 B. 邹容 C. 陈天华 D. 孙中山

12. 1927 年 4 月 18 日，南京国民政府成立，首任国民政府主席是
A. 胡汉民 B. 汪精卫 C. 蒋介石 D. 廖仲恺

13. 标志着中国抗日战争进入相持阶段的是
A. 淞沪会战结束 B. 武汉会战结束
C. 太原会战结束 D. 徐州会战结束

14. 英国资产阶级革命的领导者是
A. 资产阶级 B. 新贵族
C. 资产阶级和新贵族 D. 平民

15. 工业革命中最重要的发明是
A. 轮船 B. 珍妮纺纱机 C. 火车机车 D. 改良蒸汽机

16. 1787 年美国宪法规定立法权属于
A. 国会 B. 总统 C. 最高法院 D. 大陆会议

17. 美国内战中，林肯政府颁布的两个法令是
①《权利法案》 ②《独立宣言》 ③《宅地法》 ④《解放黑人奴隶宣言》
A. ①② B. ②③ C. ③④ D. ①④

18. 1914 年 9 月，英法联军同德军进行的大会战是
A. 马祖湖战役 B. 马恩河战役
C. 凡尔登战役 D. 索姆河战役

19. 1919 年召开的巴黎和会讨论的中心问题是
A. 建立国际联盟 B. 调整欧洲国家边界
C. 签订对德和约 D. 分配德国战争赔款

20. 美国提出马歇尔计划的根本目的是
A. 稳定欧洲资本主义制度 B. 推行“遏制共产主义”政策
C. 向苏联和东欧地区进行经济渗透 D. 帮助西欧经济复兴

二、材料分析题（本大题共 2 小题，每小题 10 分，共 20 分。）

21. 阅读下列材料

材料 1：今日和议既成，中外贸易有无交通，购买外洋器物，尤属名正言顺。购成

之后，访募覃思之士，智巧之匠，始而演习，继而试造，不过一二年，火轮船必为中外官民通行之物，可以剿发捻（太平天国运动和北方捻军起义——引者注），可以勤远略。

——引自《曾文正公全集》

材料 2：中国文武制度，事事远出西人之上，独火器万不能及。

——引自《李文忠公全书》

回答下列问题：

①以上材料是清政府中哪一派的主张？出现在什么时期？（4 分）

②材料 1 提出的学习西方先进技术的具体方法是什么？其目的是什么？（4 分）

③材料 2 作者的观点是否正确？简单说明理由。（2 分）

22. 阅读下面这段关于罗斯福新政的材料：

“只要国家仍处在危急存亡的关头，我就要求国会授予我应付危机的那种唯一的最后手段——广泛的行政权，使我可以向紧急状态宣战，就像真正有外敌入侵时一样，把那种大权授予我……”

——摘自《罗斯福就职演说》

请回答：

①罗斯福当选为美国总统是在哪一年？当时，他面临怎样的局面？（4 分）

②材料反映了罗斯福新政的最大特点是什么？结合所学知识，评价罗斯福新政。（6 分）

三、问答题（本大题共 3 小题，任选 2 题作答，每题 15 分，共 30 分。答题请注明所答小题号）

23. 简述秦统一全国后采取的巩固国家统一的经济、文化措施。
24. 简述中国抗日战争取得胜利的原因。
25. 简述第一次世界大战后华盛顿会议召开的背景、会议达成的主要条约，并简单评价这一会议。

四、论述题（本大题共 2 小题，任选 1 题作答，共 20 分。本题不预设固定答案，考生可以表达个人见解。考生答题应观点明确，并能正确引用史实加以论证。答题请注明所答小题号）

26. 晚清至民国初年，中国文化和西方文化在中国的地位发生了颠覆性的变化：中国文化的地位急剧下降，西方文化的地位显著上升。如何看待这种现象？
27. 联合国这一全球性机构是第二次世界大战结束后建立的。半个多世纪后的今天，面对新的形势，联合国该如何应对？

暨南大学、华侨大学联合招收港澳地区、台湾省、华侨、华人及其他外籍学生入学考试样题

历　史

答题卡

一、选择题

1 [A] [B] [C] [D]	6 [A] [B] [C] [D]	11 [A] [B] [C] [D]	16 [A] [B] [C] [D]
2 [A] [B] [C] [D]	7 [A] [B] [C] [D]	12 [A] [B] [C] [D]	17 [A] [B] [C] [D]
3 [A] [B] [C] [D]	8 [A] [B] [C] [D]	13 [A] [B] [C] [D]	18 [A] [B] [C] [D]
4 [A] [B] [C] [D]	9 [A] [B] [C] [D]	14 [A] [B] [C] [D]	19 [A] [B] [C] [D]
5 [A] [B] [C] [D]	10 [A] [B] [C] [D]	15 [A] [B] [C] [D]	20 [A] [B] [C] [D]

以下为非选择题答题区，必须用黑色字迹的钢笔或签字笔在指定的黑色框区域内作答，否则答案无效。

二、材料分析题（本大题共 2 小题，每小题 10 分，共 20 分。答题请注明所答小题号）

21.（10 分）

22.（10 分）

三、问答题（本大题共3小题，任选2题作答，每题15分，共30分。答题请注明所答小题号）

选做（　）题

选做（　）题

四、论述题（本大题共2小题，任选1题作答，共20分。本题不预设固定答案，考生可以表达个人见解。考生答题应观点明确，并能正确引用史实加以论证。答题请注明所答小题号）

选做（　）题

历史参考答案

一、选择题（本大题共20小题，每小题4分，共80分）

1. A　2. D　3. B　4. D　5. C　6. B　7. B　8. A　9. C　10. C

11. B　12. A　13. B　14. C　15. D　16. A　17. C　18. B　19. C　20. A

二、材料分析题（本大题共2小题，每小题10分，共20分）

21. ①洋务派的主张，出现在19世纪60年代，太平天国运动时期。(4分)
②先购买，再仿造。使清政府摆脱内忧外患，维护清朝统治。(4分)
③不正确，看不到封建制度的落后。(2分)

22. ①1932年。1929年爆发的经济危机还在不断加深。(4分)
②国家干预经济生活。(2分) 新政的实施，使美国经济缓慢地恢复过来，资本主义统治得到稳定。但它不可能从根本上消除资本主义经济危机。(4分)

三、问答题（本大题共3小题，任选2题作答，每题15分，共30分。答题请注明所答小题号）

23. ①统一度量衡，使长度、容积和重量都有统一的标准。(3分)
②统一货币，废掉六国货币，规定以秦国的圆形方孔钱作为统一的货币，通行全国。(3分)
③统一文字。把简化了的字体小篆作为标准字体，通行全国使用，秦末汉初又出现了隶书。现在的楷书便由隶书演化而来。(3分)
④统一法律。制定《秦律》，颁行全国。(3分)
⑤统一车轨，修筑驰道，以咸阳为中心，向全国辐射。(3分)

24. ①正义性的反侵略战争：中国进行的是正义的反侵略战争，且中国的抗日战争是世界反法西斯战争的重要组成部分。(3分)
②全民族抗战：抗日战争是以国共合作为基础的全民族抗战，体现了中华民族的觉醒和民族的凝聚力。从敌后战场到正面战场，从国统区到沦陷区，从国内社会各阶层到国外华侨，从汉族到少数民族，都充分体现了全民抗战的特点。(3分)
③中国共产党的中流砥柱作用：从抗日民族统一战线的倡导和建立，到全面抗战路线的制定；从敌后根据地的建立和抗日游击战争的开展，到毛泽东《论持久战》指明抗战前途；从坚持斗争求团结巩固统一战线，到抓住国际国内有利时机及时反攻胜利，都突出了中共在抗战胜利中的关键作用。(3分)
④国民党领导的正面战场、中国共产党领导的敌后战场，两大战场相互依存、相互配合，坚持到抗战胜利，成为中国抗日战争的突出特点。(3分)
⑤世界反法西斯战争的相互配合；世界反法西斯统一战线的形成和作战的相互协调

是“二战”胜利的根本原因，苏美对日作战是中国抗战决胜的有力配合。(3 分)

25. 第一次世界大战后华盛顿会议召开的背景：为协调大战后帝国主义在远东和太平洋地区的利益，1921 年 11 月，由美国倡议，中、英、法、日、意、葡、比、荷等九国代表在华盛顿举行国际会议。(3 分)

会议达成的主要条约：美、英、法、日四国条约，英、美、日、法、意五国《限制海军军备条约》，与会九国代表签订了有关中国问题的《九国公约》。(6 分)

评价：这次会议是巴黎和约的继续，它确定了战后帝国主义在远东和太平洋地区的统治秩序，完成了帝国主义对世界的重新瓜分，建立了“凡尔赛—华盛顿体系”。然而，这一体系不可能消除帝国主义之间的矛盾，因此，也就不可能长期维持下去。(6 分)

四、论述题（本大题共 2 小题，任选 1 题作答，共 20 分。本题不预设固定答案，考生可以表达个人见解。考生答题应观点明确，并能正确引用史实加以论证。答题请注明所答小题号）

论述题评分准则

分数	评分准则
18 ~ 20	立场明确，内容均衡，引用史实丰富、准确，评论详细深入，意见或议论精辟
13 ~ 17	立场清晰，内容较为均衡，能略引史实支持论点，援引史实无重大错漏，意见或议论较中肯
8 ~ 12	有一定立场，能说出自己的看法，史实及分析能力一般，援引史实有一定错漏，意见或议论切题
4 ~ 7	立场不定，有一定的看法，但史实及分析能力严重不足，援引史实大部分有错漏，意见或议论与题旨有一定关联
0 ~ 3	答案凌乱，内容贫乏，空洞无物，远离题旨

地　理

考试要求

（1）识记重要地理事物的名称和空间位置；了解涉及地理的重大时事。

（2）掌握有关地图的基本知识，具备读图、填图的技能，包括判读和分析各种地理图表所承载的信息。

（3）了解地球的宇宙环境和人类赖以生存和发展的地理环境；了解人类活动对环境的影响，理解人文环境的形成和特点，认识可持续发展的重要意义。

（4）掌握本大纲涉及的世界各区域和国家的地理特征。

（5）掌握中国地理基本特征，理解中国地理国情、基本国策。

（6）能够从题目的文字表述中获取地理信息，运用正确的地理观念，探讨、评价现实中的地理问题。

（7）能够运用基本的地理数据、地理概念、地理事物的主要特征及分布、地理原理与规律等知识，按题日要求作答。

（8）能够运用所学的地理知识和相关学科的知识，通过比较、判断、分析，阐释地理基本原理与规律。

考试范围与内容

地理科考试内容包括地球和地图、世界地理、中国地理、自然地理、人文地理五部分。具体内容如下：

一、地球和地图

1．宇宙中的地球

（1）地球的宇宙环境：地球所处的宇宙环境，太阳对地球的影响，地球上存在生命物质的条件，宇宙探测的现状和意义。

（2）地球：地球的形状和地理坐标，地球自转和公转的地理意义。

2．地图

（1）地图三要素：比例尺的运用，地图上方向的判读，常用图例、注记。

（2）地形图：海拔（绝对高度）和相对高度，等高（深）线和等高线地形图，地形剖面图及其运用。

（3）地理信息技术及其应用。

二、世界地理

1. 世界地理概况

（1）世界海陆分布：地球表面水陆面积的比例，七大洲和四大洋的位置。

（2）世界的气候：世界主要气候类型的基本特点及其分布，判别气候类型的基本方法。

（3）世界的居民：世界的人种及主要分布地区，世界主要国家及其首都，世界著名城市和港口。

（4）地区发展差异：发展中国家与发达国家的地区分布特点，联合国及其他国际组织在国际合作中的作用。

2. 世界地理分区

（1）亚洲：亚洲主要的高原、山脉、平原、河流、湖泊的名称和位置，亚洲南部三大半岛和世界最大的群岛，多样的地域文化，经济发展差异。

日本：日本的领土组成和自然环境，日本的经济特征、工业分布。

东南亚：东南亚的范围，马六甲海峡的位置，东南亚气候与农业生产，东南亚丰富的物产。

印度：印度的自然环境对农业生产和工业分布的影响。

西亚：西亚重要的地理位置，西亚石油资源。

（2）非洲：三大高原、东非大裂谷、撒哈拉沙漠的位置，气候类型南北对称分布的热带大陆，尼罗河、刚果河，丰富的资源和野生动物。

埃及：重要的地理位置，苏伊士运河的位置。

（3）欧洲：主要半岛的名称和位置，以平原为主的地形，深受大西洋影响的气候，多瑙河、莱茵河，发达的经济，欧洲联盟。

英国：英国国土的组成，工业的分布和变化。

法国：法国工农业都发达的经济，巴黎盆地。

德国：德国发达的工业，鲁尔区的工业特点。

意大利：意大利国土的组成，工业区的发展条件、特点。

俄罗斯：俄罗斯地理概况，主要工业区的分布，自然条件对经济的影响。

（4）北美洲：北美洲的地理位置和范围，北美洲的地形、气候特点，五大湖，密西西比河。

美国：美国地理位置和领土组成，丰富的资源对经济的影响，农业地区专业化及主要农业带，主要工业区，技术创新对美国经济的影响。

（5）南美洲：拉丁美洲的范围，南美洲的地形特征、气候特征，丰富的资源和特有的动植物，亚马孙河流域热带雨林的开发与保护。

巴西：发展中的工农业大国。

（6）大洋洲：大洋洲的位置和范围，岛屿的类型和成因。

澳大利亚：澳大利亚气候类型呈半环状分布，独特的动植物，主要工农业及其分布。

新西兰：新西兰领土组成，自然地理特征对经济的影响。

（7）两极地区：独特的地理位置，自然地理特征，生物资源和矿产资源。

极地考察：南极洲、北冰洋科学考察的意义，南极考察站长城站、中山站、昆仑站和泰山站的位置，北极考察站黄河站的位置。

三、中国地理

1. 疆域与人口

（1）地理位置，国土构成，行政区划。

（2）人口：中国人口的分布和增长，中国的人口政策，华侨和侨乡。

（3）民族：统一的多民族国家，中国民族的分布特点。

2. 自然环境与自然资源

（1）地形；地形的基本特征，地形对中国地理环境和经济发展的影响。

主要山脉的走向及其分布，四大高原、四大盆地、三大平原的分布及特点。

中国地震带和火山的分布，滑坡、泥石流等地质灾害与地形的关系。

（2）气候：中国冬季和夏季气温分布特点及其成因，中国降水的分布特点，冬季风和夏季风的特点，季风活动和雨带的移动，梅雨、伏旱的成因。

中国气候的主要特征，中国气候的优缺点，影响中国的台风、寒潮、旱涝灾害。

（3）河流和湖泊：主要河流的分布、水文特征及形成原因，主要湖泊。

长江、黄河、珠江概况，长江水资源的开发、利用，黄河水害及其治理，珠江水系及经济意义。

（4）自然资源：自然资源时空分布不均的特点及解决措施，南水北调，西气东输，西电东送。

中国土地资源的分布，保护中国土地资源的重要性。

中国旅游资源的多样性，中国的世界遗产，主要旅游景点：万里长城、桂林山水、杭州西湖、北京故宫、苏州园林、安徽黄山、长江三峡、台湾日月潭、承德避暑山庄、陕西秦陵兵马俑。

（5）区域差异：中国三大自然区的空间位置和基本特征，东部季风区内部的差异，自然区域差异对人类活动的影响。

香港特别行政区和澳门特别行政区的位置，两地经济的异同点。

四、自然地理

1. 大气

（1）大气的组成和垂直分层：大气的组成及大气主要成分的作用，对流层、平流层、电离层对人类活动的影响。

（2）气温：大气的热状况，气温的日变化和年变化，气温水平分布的一般规律。

（3）降水：降水类型及其原因，世界降水的分布状况。

(4) 天气：锋面、气旋（低气压）和反气旋（高气压）等天气系统的特点。
(5) 气候：气压带、风带的形成和分布，太阳辐射、大气环流和地面状况对气候的影响。
(6) 大气环境：地球温室效应、臭氧层遭破坏和酸雨危害等大气环境问题，大气环境保护。

2. 地球上的水
(1) 水循环：水循环的主要环节及其地理意义。
(2) 海洋水：海水温度和盐度，洋流分布规律及对地理环境的影响，海洋资源的开发，海洋环境的保护。
(3) 陆地水：陆地主要水体类型，河流的补给，地下水的来源和类型。

3. 地壳的变动
(1) 地球的内部圈层：地球的圈层结构，地球内部的圈层构造和划分依据。
(2) 地壳运动：板块构造学说的主要内容，板块运动对地表的影响，地壳运动的类型及主要表现形式，地表形态变化的内、外力因素，地质构造。
(3) 主要地质灾害及其防御，世界地震和火山带的分布。

4. 生物与地理环境
(1) 生物与地理环境：生物在地理环境中的作用，植物的分布与环境的关系，生物对地理环境的指示作用。
(2) 生态系统与生态平衡。

5. 地理环境的整体性和地域分异
(1) 自然地理要素在地理环境形成和演变中的作用。
(2) 地理环境的整体性，地理环境的地域分异规律，地理环境对人类的影响。

五、人文地理

1. 人口与城市
(1) 人口：不同人口增长模式的主要特点及地区分布，世界人口的分布，人口迁移的主要原因，环境承载力与人口合理容量的区别。
(2) 城市：自然、经济、社会等因素对城市发展的影响，城市的空间结构及其形成原因，城市化的过程和特点，城市化对地理环境的影响。
(3) 地域文化对人口和城市的影响。

2. 生产活动与地域联系
(1) 农业：农业区位因素，主要农业地域类型的分布及其特点，中国农业发展的条件，三类不同地区的农业生产。
(2) 工业：工业区位因素，工业布局的发展变化，工业地域的形成条件与发展特点，中国主要工业基地。
(3) 地域联系：人类活动地域联系的主要方式（交通运输、通信、商业、服务业等）。

交通运输：主要交通运输方式及其特点，交通对聚落空间形态和商业网点布局的影响，中国主要交通运输线、铁路枢纽、航空中心、港口的分布。

商业贸易：影响商业中心形成的区位因素，国际上主要的贸易组织，中国主要商业中心。

3. 人类与地理环境的协调发展

（1）区域地理环境与人类活动：不同区域自然环境、人类活动的差异，不同发展阶段地理环境对人类生产和生活方式的影响。

（2）可持续发展：人地关系思想的历史演变，人类所面临的主要环境问题，协调人地关系的主要途径，中国的可持续发展战略。

（3）中国典型区域存在的环境与发展问题及有关的治理保护措施。

考试形式

考试采用闭卷、书面作答的形式，考试时间为 120 分钟，试卷满分为 150 分。

试卷结构与题型

（1）试卷题型：试卷包括单项选择题，填空题，读图、填图题，综合题四种题型。单项选择题分值为 60 分，填空题分值为 20 分，读图、填图题分值为 20 分，综合题分值为 50 分。

（2）试题难度：试卷难易程度适中，试卷重点考查考生对地理基础知识与基本技能的掌握程度和综合运用所学知识分析、解决问题的能力。

（3）考查知识分布：地球和地图约占 15%，自然地理约占 40%（含区域地理），人文地理约占 45%（含区域地理）。

考生复习参考资料

1. 黄小黎，蔡贤榜. 暨南大学、华侨大学联合招收港澳地区、台湾省、华侨、华人及其他外籍学生入学考试复习丛书 · 地理. 广州：暨南大学出版社，2015.

2. 黄小黎，蔡贤榜. 暨南大学、华侨大学两校联招及全国联招 2004—2011 年试题详解丛书 · 地理. 广州：暨南大学出版社，2013.

3. 黄小黎，蔡贤榜. 暨南大学、华侨大学及全国联招考试模拟试题丛书 · 地理. 广州：暨南大学出版社，2013.

样卷

暨南大学、华侨大学联合招收港澳地区、台湾省、华侨、华人及其他外籍学生入学考试样题

科目：地　理

答卷时间：120 分钟

一、单项选择题（本大题共 20 小题，选对一小题得 3 分，共 60 分）

读右图完成 1 ~3 题。

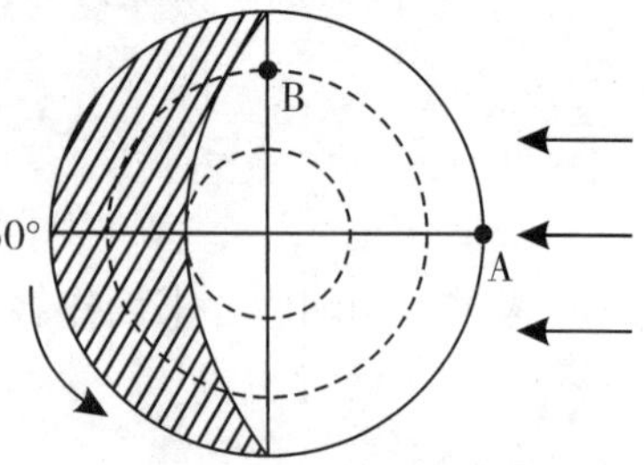

1. 此时，广州：
   A. 高温多雨
   B. 昼短夜长
   C. 东北风盛行
   D. 风高物燥
2. 如果 A 点的区时是某日 12 时，北京时间可能是：
   A. 当日 16 时　　B. 当日 10 时
   C. 当日 4 时　　D. 当日 22 时
3. 这一天，下列现象不可信的是：
   A. 亚欧大陆等温线向北凸出　　B. 潘帕斯草原一片嫩绿
   C. 地中海天气晴朗　　D. 尼罗河的河口处海水盐度最低
4. 下面四幅图中关于 B 相对 A 的方向判断排列顺序，正确的是：

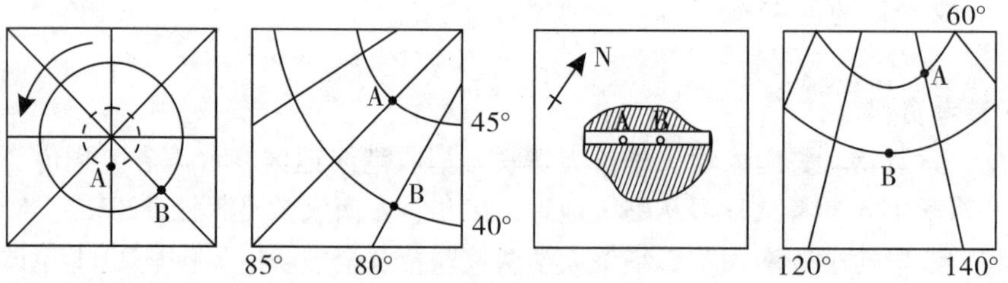

①　　②　　③　　④

   A. 西南、东北、西北、西北　　B. 西北、东北、西南、西北
   C. 西北、西南、东北、西北　　D. 东南、东南、东北、西南
5. 在地图上，赤道上的甲乙两地相距 33.3 厘米，地方时相差 4 小时，则下述说法正确的是：
   A. 该地图比例尺为 1∶10 000 000
   B. 该地图上与甲乙两地图上距离相同的两点，地方时也相差 4 小时

C. 在该区域1∶10 000 000的新地图上，图幅面积比旧图增大了3倍

D. 该地图比例尺比1∶20 000 000地图比例尺小

6. 读右图判断分析，叙述正确的是：

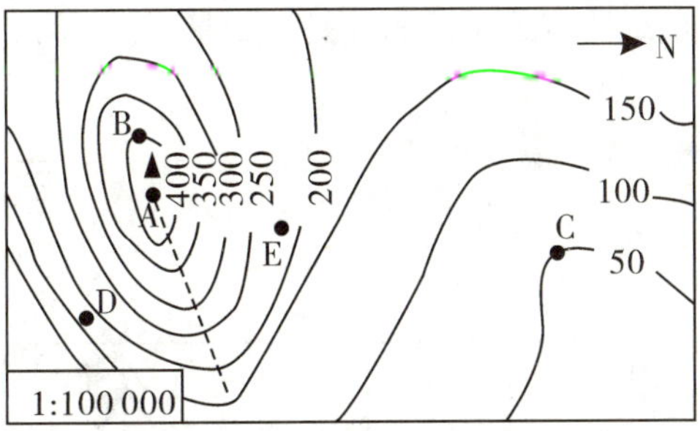

A. A表示的是山顶，虚线表示的是山谷

B. B、C两地的温差约为2.1℃

C. C处为盆地，E处为山脊

D. D坡为缓坡，可开垦梯田

7. 当太阳直射点位于赤道时：

A. 北回归线以南的地区，正午太阳位于北方

B. 北极圈以北有极昼现象

C. 赤道正午太阳高度达一年最大

D. 正常年份，中国的雨带已经北移到华北

8. 关于非洲地理的叙述，正确的是：

A. 地形以高原为主，平均海拔高度居各洲之首

B. 非洲的人口和国家、地区数目居世界各大陆之首

C. 绕道好望角的航线被西方国家称为“海上生命线”

D. 热带经济作物的种类和产量最多

9. 2014年加入联合国《世界遗产名录》名单的是：

A. 大运河　　B. 丹霞山　　C. 九寨沟　　D. 神农架

10. 下列关于东南亚与南亚地理特征不同点的叙述，正确的是：

A. 东南亚以白色人种为主，而南亚以黄色人种为主

B. 东南亚适宜天然橡胶生长，而南亚有利于棉花种植

C. 南亚产业属于资源密集型，而东南亚产业属于技术密集型

D. 南亚是世界上华人华侨聚集之地，而东南亚华人华侨相对较少

下表是三个城市的气候资料，据此回答11～13题。

城市		①	②	③
平均气温（℃）	1月	5	11	21
	7月	29	27	26
平均降水量（mm）	1月	47	75	1
	7月	150	5	610

11. 城市①所处自然带的典型植被类型是：

A. 热带雨林　　B. 亚寒带针叶林

C. 亚热带常绿硬叶林　　D. 亚热带常绿阔叶林

12. ②所属的气候类型，适宜生长的水果是：

A. 柑橘　　B. 香蕉　　C. 椰子　　D. 荔枝

13. 城市③所属的气候类型是：

A. 温带季风气候　　B. 热带季风气候

C. 温带大陆性气候　　D. 热带沙漠气候

下图为中国四座重要山脉，读后回答 14～16 题。

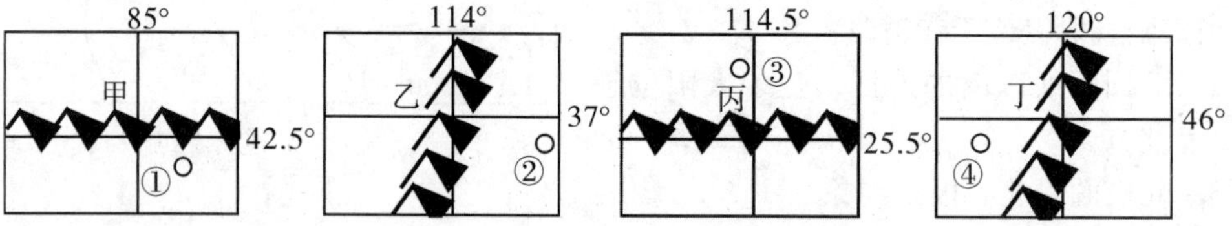

14. 四座山脉中两侧都是盆地的是：

A. 甲　　B. 乙　　C. 丙　　D. 丁

15. 属于中国季风区与非季风区界线的山脉为：

A. 甲　　B. 乙　　C. 丙　　D. 丁

16. 下列说法中错误的是：

A. ①地有中国重要的商品棉基地　　B. ②地水土流失严重

C. ③地以平原丘陵为主　　D. ④地地表平坦，一望无际

17. 下列旅游胜地与其所在省区及其简称组合，正确的是：

A. 黄山—浙江省—浙　　B. 洞庭湖—江西省—赣

C. 鼎湖山—广东省—粤　　D. 张家界—湖南省—湖

18. 关于澳大利亚的叙述，正确的是：

A. 南半球中面积最大、人口最多的国家

B. 西部是南北纵贯的大分水岭，中部是平原，东部是广阔低矮的高原

C. 农牧产品的出口收入大于工矿产品的出口收入

D. 气候干燥，沙漠和半沙漠分布很广

19. 关于地壳运动的叙述，正确的是：

A. 外力作用造成地势的高低起伏和海陆变迁

B. 升降运动常造成巨大的褶皱山系

C. 在地壳的发展过程中，内力起主导作用

D. 珠江三角洲是地壳的水平运动造成的

20. 以下关于自然条件与城市区位的叙述，正确的是：

A. 中国和世界上的城市大多数都位于平原地区

B. 世界城市主要分布于中、低纬度地区，中国城市多分布于半干旱、半湿润地区

C. 河流的入海口和发源地，都是城市建设的最优地点

D. 中国北方城市都是沿江河湖泊发育壮大起来的

二、填空题（本大题共20个空格，每填对一空格得1分，共20分。请将答案填写在答题卡相应空格内）

21. 我国西部地区地形以高原、山地和________为主。我国东部地区南北分界线是________—________，此线以南的气候类型是______________，此线以北的主要植被类型是______________。

22. 我国面积最大的岛屿是________，岛上面积最大的湖泊是________。我国面积最大的沙漠位于________盆地。位于东北平原的两个商品粮基地是________、________。

23. 我国于1985年在乔治王岛建立了________南极考察站；1989年在南极大陆边缘建立了________南极考察站；2008年在南极内陆冰盖最高点建立了________南极考察站；2014年在东南极内陆冰盖腹地建立了________南极考察站；2004年在挪威斯匹次卑尔根群岛建立了________北极考察站。

24. 世界工业地带的分布很不均衡，主要集中在北半球中纬度地区。________工业地带是世界上最大的工业地带，________工业地带是现代工业的发源地，东欧工业地带是________型重工业地带，日本太平洋沿岸工业地带是世界著名的________型工业地带，亚洲东部沿海工业地带的工业类型正在逐渐从________密集型向技术密集型过渡。

三、读图、填图题（本大题共3小题，每空格1分，共20分。请将答案填写在答题卡相应空格内）

25. 读“世界上两个国家的示意图”，完成下列内容。

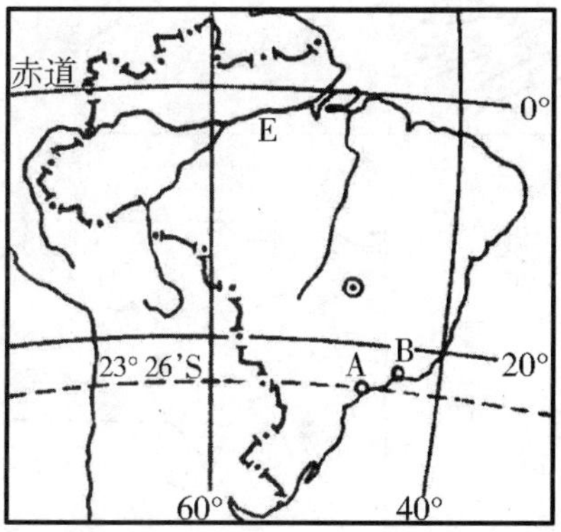

甲

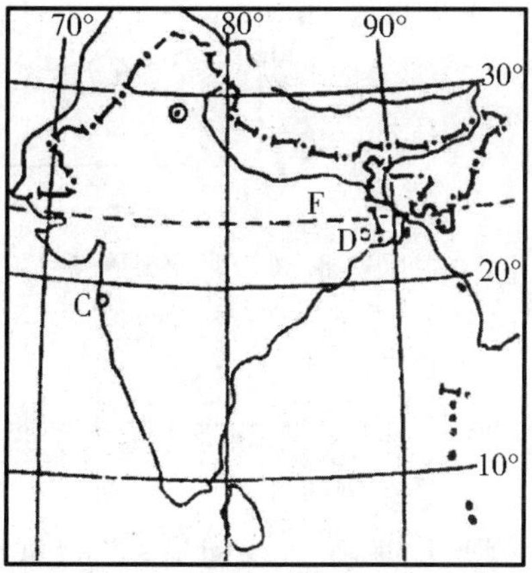

乙

（1）甲、乙两幅图比较，面积较大的是______图。

（2）B城市是2016年第31届奥林匹克运动会主办的城市___________。C城市是该国最大的海港____________。

（3）甲图中的 E 河流是____________，E 所在地区人口稀少，属于______气候，终年________。

（4）乙图中的 F 河流是____________，该河的三角洲是世界黄麻的最大产区。

26. 铁路是城市之间的纽带。厦深铁路于 2013 年建成通车，从深圳到厦门运行从原来 14 小时缩短为 3 小时。贵广高铁于 2014 年建成通车，使贵阳与广州的铁路运行时间由 20 小时缩短至 4 小时左右。读下图，回答问题：

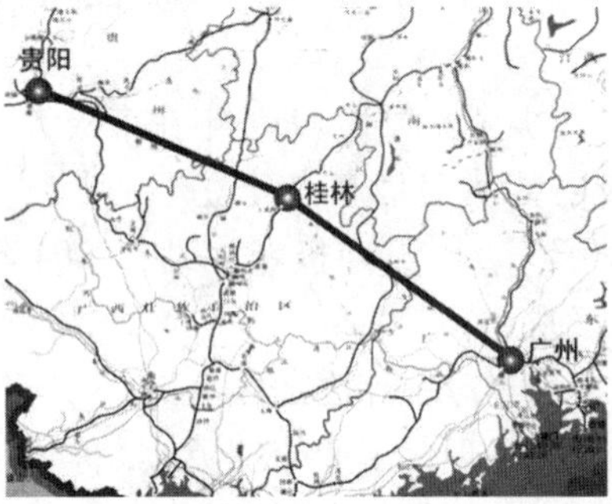

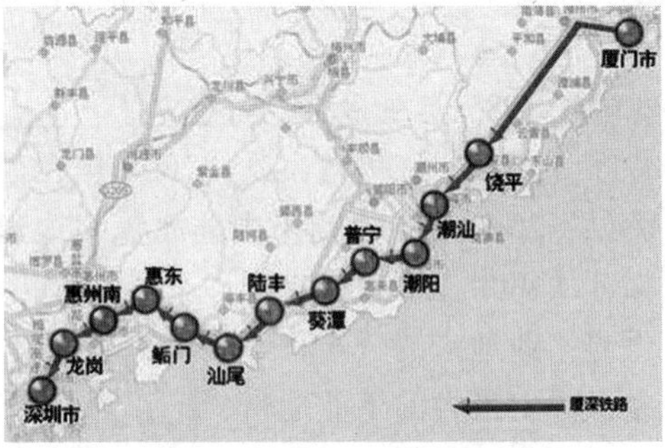

（1）贵广高铁经过的省级行政区是__________、____________、广东省。

（2）厦深铁路经过下图的地质构造区，甲处的地质构造是____________；乙处的地质构造是____________；应在____________（填甲、乙或丙）建隧道。

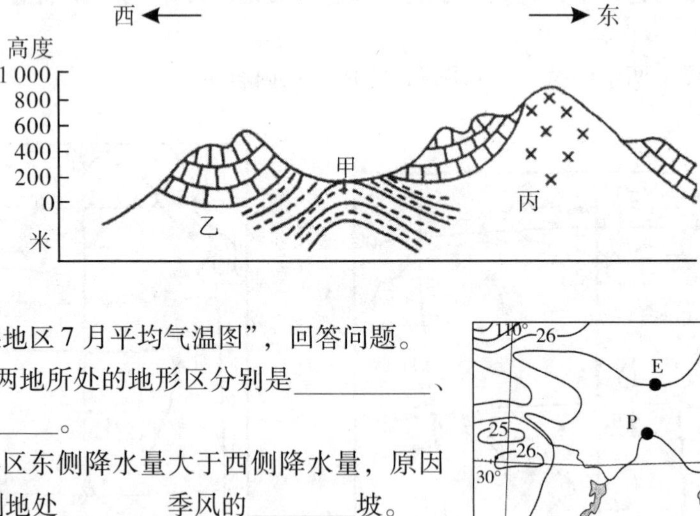

27. 读“中国某地区 7 月平均气温图”，回答问题。

（1）A、B 两地所处的地形区分别是__________、__________。

（2）B 地形区东侧降水量大于西侧降水量，原因是东侧地处________季风的________坡。

（3）E 地等温线向低纬突出，主要受_______影响；

F 地等温线大致与海岸线平行，主要受________影响。

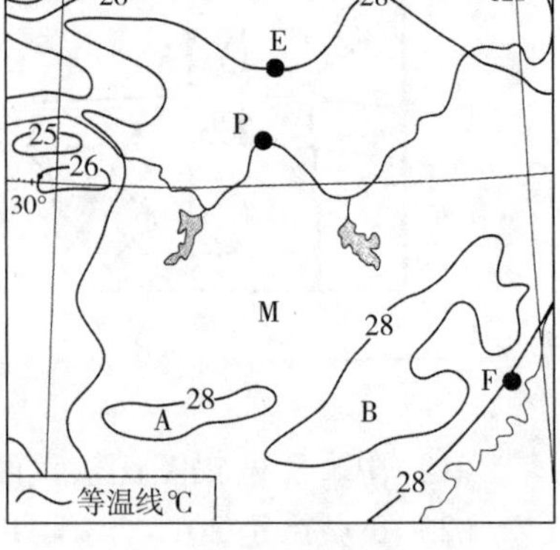

（4）P 城市是长江中游重要城市＿＿＿＿＿＿市。

（5）M 地在工业发展中可能出现的主要环境问题是＿＿＿＿＿。

四、综合题（本大题共 3 小题，共 50 分。请将答案填写在答题卡相应空格内）

28．读“俄罗斯地形图”，回答下列问题。（18 分）

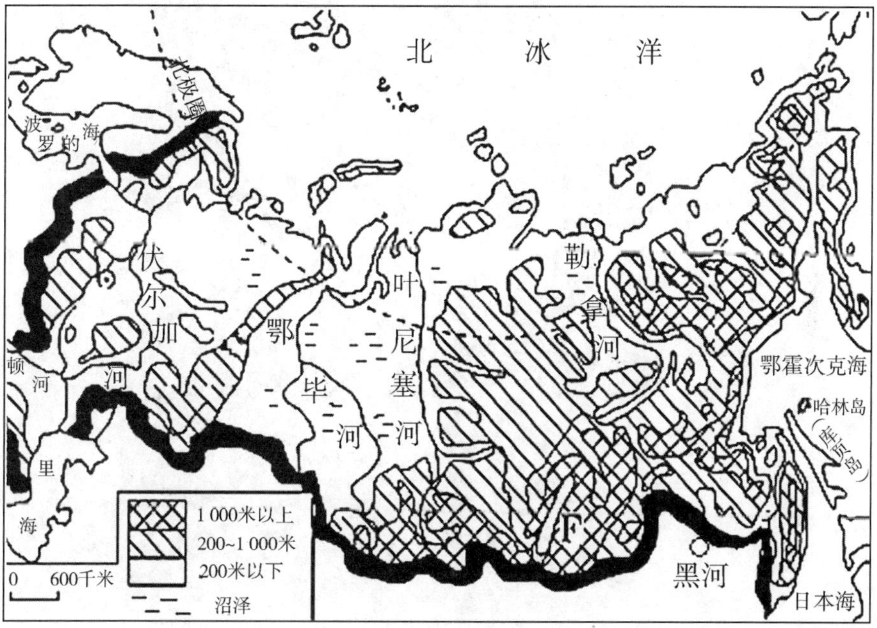

俄罗斯地形图

（1）简述俄罗斯地形特征。

（2）说明俄罗斯湿地资源丰富的原因。

（3）河流的两岸及中下游平原大多是重要的农业区，但俄罗斯西伯利亚三大河流的下游却几乎没有农田，分析该地种植业不发达的主要原因。

（4）简要评价俄罗斯亚洲部分发展经济的自然条件。

29. 中国南水北调工程是实现水资源优化配置、促进经济社会可持续发展的重大战略性基础设施。南水北调中线一期工程于2014年12月12日正式通水。回答下列问题。（16分）

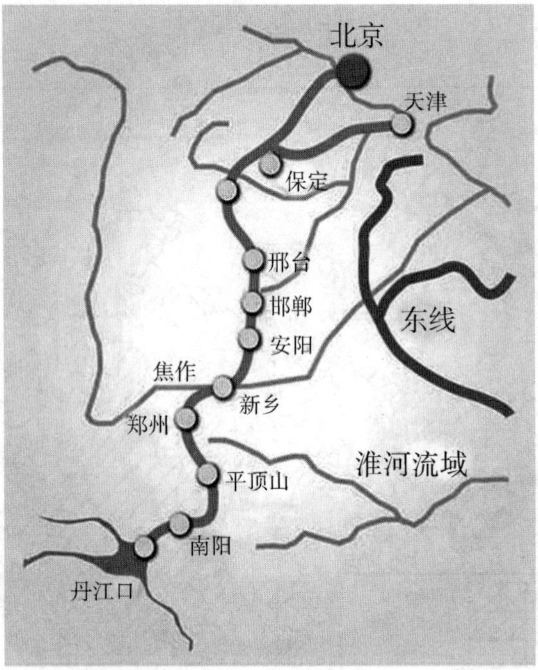

（1）中国华北地区缺水的原因是什么？

（2）中线工程的优点。

（3）分析南水北调工程的意义。

30. 分析上海成为中国最大城市和港口的区位因素。（16分）

暨南大学、华侨大学联合招收港澳地区、台湾省、华侨、华人及其他外籍学生入学考试样题

地　理

答题卡

一、单项选择题

1 [A] [B] [C] [D]	6 [A] [B] [C] [D]	11 [A] [B] [C] [D]	16 [A] [B] [C] [D]
2 [A] [B] [C] [D]	7 [A] [B] [C] [D]	12 [A] [B] [C] [D]	17 [A] [B] [C] [D]
3 [A] [B] [C] [D]	8 [A] [B] [C] [D]	13 [A] [B] [C] [D]	18 [A] [B] [C] [D]
4 [A] [B] [C] [D]	9 [A] [B] [C] [D]	14 [A] [B] [C] [D]	19 [A] [B] [C] [D]
5 [A] [B] [C] [D]	10 [A] [B] [C] [D]	15 [A] [B] [C] [D]	20 [A] [B] [C] [D]

以下为非选择题答题区，必须用黑色字迹的钢笔或签字笔在指定的黑色框区域内作答，否则答案无效。

二、填空题（本大题共 20 个空格，每填对一空格得 1 分，共 20 分。请将答案填写在答题卡相应空格内）

21. ________　________　________　________　________

22. ________　________　________　________　________

23. ________　________　________　________　________

24. ________　________　________　________　________

三、读图、填图题（本大题共 3 小题，每空格 1 分，共 20 分。请将答案填写在答题卡相应空格内）

25. （1）________

（2）________　________

（3）________　________　________

（4）________

26. （1）________　________

（2）________　________　________

27. （1）________　________

(2) ________________ ________________

(3) ________________ ________________

(4) ________________

(5) ________________

四、综合题（本大题共 3 小题，共 50 分。请将答案填写在答题卡相应空格内）

28. (1) ________________

(2) ________________

(3) ________________

(4) ________________

29. (1) ________________

(2) ________________

(3) ________________

30. ________________

地理参考答案

一、单项选择题（本大题共 20 小题，选对一小题得 3 分，共 60 分）

1. A 2. C 3. B 4. D 5. C 6. B 7. C 8. C 9. A 10. B

11. D 12. A 13. B 14. A 15. D 16. B 17. C 18. D 19. C 20. A

二、填空题（本大题共 20 个空格，每填对一空格得 1 分，共 20 分）

21. 盆地 秦岭 淮河 亚热带季风气候 落叶阔叶林
22. 台湾岛 日月潭 塔里木 三江平原 松嫩平原
23. 长城 中山 昆仑 泰山 黄河
24. 北美 西欧 资源 临海 劳动力

三、读图、填图题（本大题共 3 小题，每空格 1 分，共 20 分）

25. （1）甲

（2）里约热内卢 孟买

（3）亚马孙河 热带雨林 高温多雨

（4）恒河

26. （1）贵州省 广西壮族自治区

（2）背斜 向斜 甲

27. （1）南岭 武夷山脉

（2）东南 迎风

（3）地形 海洋

（4）武汉

（5）酸雨

四、综合题（本大题共 3 小题，共 50 分）

28. （1）①地势东高西低，南高北低，总体较平坦；(3 分)

②以叶尼塞河为界，西部主要是平原，东部为高原山地。(3 分)

（2）①地势低平，排水不畅；(1 分)

②气温低，蒸发弱；(1 分)

③有凌汛现象，会造成下游河水泛滥；(1 分)

④永久性冻土广布，形成不透水层，表层的水分难以下渗。(1 分)

（3）①三大河流沿岸平原地区纬度位置高，热量条件差，不适宜农作物生长；(2 分)

②河流沿岸沼泽广布，无法进行农耕。(2 分)

（4）①优势条件：面积广大；自然资源丰富。(2 分)
②劣势条件：气候严寒；冻土广布；河流与海域的结冰期长。(2 分)

29.（1）缺水的原因
①自然原因：华北地区属于半湿润地区，降水少，蒸发量大；且降水集中在7、8 月份；河流湖泊少，积蓄水量少，许多雨水都以洪水形式流入海洋；特别是春季干旱严重。(4 分)
②人为原因：华北地区工农业发达；人口稠密；需水量大，人均径流量少；污染和浪费现象严重。(4 分)

（2）中线工程的优点：中线工程从长江支流汉江上的丹江口水库引水，沿黄淮海平原西部边缘布设自流输水总干渠，终点为北京、天津。为鄂、豫、冀、津、京五省市提供城市生活、工业、农业及其他用水。中线工程具有水质好、水量大，覆盖面广，自南向北自流输水，自西向东自流供水，供水机动灵活的优点，是解决华北水资源危机的最佳方案。(4 分)

（3）南水北调工程的意义：促进受水区经济发展，对于实现国民经济可持续发展，恢复、保持生态环境；缓解城乡争水、地区争水、工农业争水的矛盾；增加生活用水和生产用水，有利于各种生物生长，美化环境；缓解地下水水位下降趋势，控制地面沉降。(4 分)

30.（1）上海市的区位因素
①自然地理区位：位于长江中下游平原，地形平坦；亚热带季风气候区，温暖湿润；长江入海口，水源丰富。(4 分)
②经济地理区位：水陆交通便利；丰富的农副产品；宽广的经济腹地；充足的商品供应，广阔的消费市场；科技发达、人口稠密；长江三角洲的中心城市。(4 分)

（2）上海港的区位因素
①自然条件优越：位于长江入海口，大陆沿海航线的居中位置，河港、海港兼备；有长江和黄浦江为港口提供充足的淡水和轮船停泊的空间；三角洲地势平坦开阔，筑港条件好。(4 分)
②经济腹地广阔且发达，交通非常便利；有上海市为依托。(4 分)

物　理

考试要求

（1）理解能力：理解物理概念、规律的确切含义，理解物理规律的适用条件，以及它们在简单情况下的应用；能够清楚地认识概念和规律的表达形式（包括文字表述和数学表达）；能够鉴别关于概念和规律的似是而非的说法；理解相关知识的区别和联系。

（2）推理能力：能够根据已知的知识和物理事实、条件，对物理问题进行逻辑推理和论证，得出正确的结论或作出正确的判断，并能把推理过程正确地表达出来。

（3）分析综合能力：能够独立地对所遇到的问题进行具体分析，弄清其中的物理状态、物理过程和原因，找出其中起重要作用的因素及有关条件；能够把一个复杂的问题分解为若干较简单的问题，找出它们之间的联系；能够理论联系实际，运用物理知识综合解决所遇到的问题。

（4）应用数学处理物理问题的能力：能够根据具体问题列出物理量之间的关系式，进行推导和求解，并根据结果得出物理结论；必要时能运用几何图形、函数图像进行表达、分析。

（5）实验能力：能独立完成“考试范围与内容”中所列的实验，能明确实验目的，能理解实验原理和方法，能控制实验条件，会使用仪器，会观察、分析实验现象，会记录、处理实验数据，并得出结论；能灵活地运用已学过的物理理论、实验方法和实验仪器去处理问题。

关于考试要求的几点说明：

（1）本大纲既包含理论知识，也包含实验知识。但考试时，实验知识只要求书面作答，不要求考生在考场动手做实验。

（2）本大纲所涉及的数学知识包括三角、代数、几何、解析几何等普通数学知识。微积分不作要求。

（3）一般采用国际单位制（SI），也要求熟悉下列符号：μ（微）、m（毫）、k（千）、cm（厘米）。还要求会用下列单位：Å（埃）、°（度，指角度）、℃（摄氏度）、eV（电子伏特）、kWh（千瓦小时）、atm（标准大气压）、cmHg（厘米汞柱），以及年、月、日、小时、分、秒。

（4）考试答卷时，物理专用名词可以写成英文。

考试范围与内容

考试内容包括力学、热学、电磁学、光学、原子物理学五部分及实验。

一、力学

1. 运动学

（1）质点，参考系，标量和矢量。

（2）位移和路程，速度，加速度。

（3）匀速直线运动，匀变速直线运动，自由落体运动，竖直上抛运动。

（4）运动的图示法（$s-t$ 图和 $v-t$ 图）。

（5）曲线运动，平抛运动。

（6）匀速圆周运动，线速度和角速度，向心加速度。

2. 力和力的平衡

（1）力，力的合成与分解，重力。

（2）弹性力，胡克定律。

（3）摩擦力，静摩擦，滑动摩擦和滑动摩擦系数。

（4）共点力作用下物体的平衡。

3. 牛顿运动定律和万有引力定律

（1）牛顿第一定律，惯性。

（2）牛顿第二定律，质量与重量。

（3）牛顿第三定律。

（4）万有引力定律。

（5）向心力，天体运动（限于圆轨道）。

4. 功和能

（1）功，功率。

（2）动能，势能，重力势能，弹簧的势能（定性）。

（3）闭合系统中能量转换的守恒关系：动能定理。

（4）机械能守恒定律。

5. 动量

（1）动量，冲量。

（2）动量守恒定律。

（3）碰撞（限于一维），反冲。

6. 振动

（1）弹簧振子，简谐运动及图像。

（2）振幅、周期和频率。

（3）单摆的周期公式。

（4）受迫振动和共振现象（定性）。

7. 波
(1) 波的形成条件，横波，纵波。
(2) 波速、波长、周期（频率）以及三者的关系，波形图。
(3) 波的干涉和波的衍射（定性）。

二、热学

1. 温度和热量
(1) 摄氏温标，热力学温标。
(2) 热量，比热容。
2. 物态的改变
(1) 熔化和凝固。
(2) 汽化和液化。
(3) 熔化热，汽化热。
(4) 升华和凝华。
3. 分子动理论
(1) 分子动理论，布朗运动，分子力。
(2) 分子的动能，分子的势能，物体的内能。
(3) 热力学第一定律，第一类永动机是不可能的（定性）。
4. 理想气体
(1) 理想气体，气体的状态和状态参量。
(2) 温度和压强的微观解释。
(3) 气体的三大实验定律，理想气体状态方程。
5. 能源的开发和利用，能源的利用与环境保护（定性）。

三、电磁学

1. 静电场
(1) 电荷，点电荷，电荷守恒，库仑定律。
(2) 电场强度，电场线，匀强电场，场强叠加原理。
(3) 电势差和电势，等势面。
(4) 电场强度和电势差的关系（限于匀强电场）。
(5) 带电粒子在匀强电场中的运动。
(6) 电容器，电容，平行板电容器的电容与板面积和板间距的关系（定性）。
2. 直流电
(1) 电流强度，欧姆定律，电阻，电阻定律。
(2) 电阻的串联和并联。
(3) 电源的电动势和内电阻，闭合电路欧姆定律。
(4) 电功和电功率，电阻上消耗的功率。

3. 磁场

(1) 磁场的方向，磁感应强度，磁场线。

(2) 电流的磁效应。

(3) 通电流的长直导线、圆环和螺线管的磁场线分布，右手螺旋定则。

4. 磁场对运动电荷的作用

(1) 安培力，左手定则。

(2) 洛伦兹力，运动电荷在匀强磁场中的运动（限 v 垂直于 B 的情况）。

(3) 质谱仪（定性），回旋加速器（定性）。

5. 电磁感应和交流电

(1) 电磁感应现象。

(2) 法拉第电磁感应定律，楞次定律。

(3) 自感现象。

(4) 互感现象，变压器原理。

(5) 交流发电机原理。

(6) 正弦交流电的波形，有效值，峰值。

(7) 远距离电能的输送。

6. 电磁振荡和电磁波

(1) 振荡电路（定性）。

(2) 电磁波，电磁波的波速，电磁波谱。

四、光学

1. 几何光学

(1) 反射定律，平面镜成像。

(2) 折射定律，折射率，折射率与光速的关系，三棱镜折射，色散。

(3) 全反射，临界角，光路的可逆性，光导纤维（定性）。

(4) 透镜成像及作图法。

2. 光的干涉和衍射

(1) 光的电磁学说。

(2) 光的干涉，杨氏双缝实验（定性），薄膜干涉（定性）。

(3) 光的衍射（定性）。

3. 光电效应

(1) 爱因斯坦光电方程，普朗克恒量。

(2) 光的波粒二象性。

(3) 激光的特性及应用（定性）。

五、原子物理学

1. 原子

（1）发射光谱和吸收光谱，线状光谱和连续光谱。

（2）原子的核式结构，卢瑟福散射实验（定性）。

（3）氢原子的玻尔模型。

2. 原子核

（1）天然放射现象，半衰期。

（2）原子核的人为嬗变，原子核的组成。

（3）放射性同位素。

（4）核反应方程，核能，核的裂变，核的聚变。

（5）质能关系式。

（6）放射性污染及防护（定性）。

六、实验

（1）基本测量（游标卡尺、螺旋测微器和温度计的使用和读数）。

（2）打点计时器或数据收集器的使用：测匀变速直线运动的加速度。

（3）验证力的平行四边形定则。

（4）验证牛顿第二定律。

（5）验证机械能守恒定律

（6）研究单摆的振动周期。

（7）描绘小电珠的伏安特性曲线。

（8）测电源的电动势和内电阻。

（9）用电压表和电流表测电阻。

（10）测定玻璃的折射率。

（11）用双缝干涉测光的波长。

命题要求

以能力测试为主导，考查考生对基础知识、基本技能的掌握程度和运用所学知识分析、解决具体问题的能力。注意理论联系实际，关注科学技术和社会经济发展。重视对考生科学素养的考查。

考试形式

考试采用闭卷、书面笔答的形式，考试时间为120分钟，试卷满分为150分。

试卷结构与题型

（1）试卷中各部分内容（包括有关的实验）所占的比例如下：

力学	30%
热学	10%
电磁学	30%
光学	10%
原子物理学	10%
实验	10%

（2）试卷分三部分。第一部分为选择题，第二部分为填空题，第三部分为计算题。其中计算题分必做题和选做题。三种题型所占比例如下：选择题约占 40%，填空题约占 20%，计算题约占 40%。

（3）试题难度：试卷包括容易题、中等难度题和难题，以中等难度题为主。

考生复习参考资料

1. 姚蓓，李莹. 暨南大学、华侨大学联合招收港澳地区、台湾省、华侨、华人及其他外籍学生入学考试复习丛书·物理. 广州：暨南大学出版社，2015.
2. 姚蓓，李莹. 暨南大学、华侨大学两校联招及全国联招 2004—2011 年试题详解丛书·物理. 广州：暨南大学出版社，2013.
3. 姚蓓，李莹. 暨南大学、华侨大学及全国联招考试模拟试题丛书·物理. 广州：暨南大学出版社，2013.

样卷

暨南大学、华侨大学联合招收港澳地区、台湾省、华侨、华人及其他外籍学生入学考试样题

科目：物　理

答卷时间：120 分钟

一、选择题（60 分。**以下各小题中只有一个答案是正确的，把你认为正确的答案分别填入答题卡中。每小题选对的给 4 分，多选、错选或不选的不给分**）

1. 甲乙两汽车从同一车站出发，甲先出发，乙后出发，当乙车追上甲车时，两车运动相同的物理量是(　　)。

   A. 加速度　　B. 速度　　C. 位移　　D. 时间

2. 关于力的下述说法正确的是(　　)。

   A. 力是物体对物体的相互作用
   B. 只有直接接触的物体间才有力的作用
   C. 力可以离开物体而独立存在
   D. 力的大小可以用天平测量

3. 体育课上，体育老师在讲解接篮球的技巧时，经常这样描述：当接迎面飞来的篮球时，手接触到球以后，两臂随球后引至胸前把球接住。这样做的目的是(　　)。

   A. 减小篮球的冲量
   B. 减小篮球的动量变化
   C. 增大篮球的动量变化
   D. 减小篮球的动量变化率

4. 一个物体以角速度 ω 做匀速圆周运动时，下列说法中正确的是(　　)。

   A. 轨道半径越大线速度越小
   B. 轨道半径越大线速度越大
   C. 轨道半径越大周期越大
   D. 轨道半径越大周期越小

5. 做简谐振动的质点，在通过平衡位置处时，下列物理量具有最大值的是(　　)。

   A. 加速度　　B. 速度　　C. 位移　　D. 回复力

6. 用一个内阻不计的电源和三根电热丝加热一壶水，已知电热丝的电阻 $R_1 = R_2 > R_3$，则加热最快的方法是(　　)。

   A. 三根电热丝并联
   B. 三根电热丝串联
   C. R_1、R_2并联再与 R_3串联
   D. R_2、R_3并联再与 R_1串联

7. 关于磁场和磁感线，下列叙述中正确的是(　　)。

   A. 磁感线可以形象地描述磁场的强弱和方向，其每一点的磁场方向在该处粒子运动的方向上
   B. 磁极间的相互作用是通过磁场产生的
   C. 磁感线总是从磁体的 N 极指向 S 极
   D. 磁感线就是磁场中碎铁屑磁化后排列成的曲线

8. 如图所示，水平绝缘面上一个带电荷量为 $+q$ 的小带电体处于垂直于纸面向里的匀

强磁场中，磁感应强度为 B，小带电体的质量为 m，为了使它对水平绝缘面恰好无压力，应该(　　)。

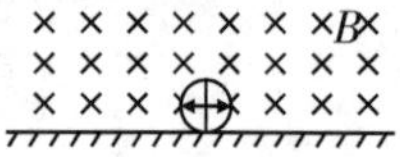

A. 使 B 的数值增大

B. 使磁场以速率 $v=\frac{mg}{qB}$ 向上移动

C. 使磁场以速率 $v=\frac{mg}{qB}$ 向左移动

D. 使磁场以速率 $v=\frac{mg}{qB}$ 向右移动

9. 电场强度 E 的定义式为 $E=\frac{F}{q}$，库仑定律的表达式为 $F=k\frac{q_1q_2}{r^2}$，下列说法中错误的是(　　)。

A. $E=\frac{F}{q}$ 也适用于点电荷产生的电场

B. $E=\frac{F}{q}$ 中的 F 是放入电场中的电荷所受的力，q 是放入电场中的电荷的电荷量

C. $E=\frac{F}{q}$ 中的 F 是放入电场中的电荷所受的力，q 是产生电场的电荷的电荷量

D. $F=k\frac{q_1q_2}{r^2}$ 中，$k\frac{q_2}{r^2}$ 是点电荷 q_2 产生的电场在点电荷 q_1 处的场强大小；而 $k\frac{q_1}{r^2}$ 是点电荷 q_1 产生的电场在点电荷 q_2 处的场强大小

10. 一个矩形线圈在匀强磁场中匀速转动时产生的交变电流的电动势为 $e=220\sqrt{2}\sin100\pi t\text{V}$，那么(　　)。

A. 该交变电流的频率是 100Hz

B. 当 $t=0$ 时，通过线圈的磁通量恰好为零

C. 该交流电电动势的有效值是 $220\sqrt{2}\text{V}$

D. 当 $t=\frac{1}{200}\text{s}$ 时，e 有最大值

11. 下列说法中正确的是(　　)。

A. 用 X 光机透视人体是利用光电效应

B. 用分光镜观测光谱是利用光折射时的色散现象

C. 光导纤维传输信号是利用光的干涉现象

D. 门镜可以扩大视野是利用光的衍射现象

12. 对一定量的气体，下列说法中正确的是(　　)。

A. 气体的体积是所有气体分子的体积之和

B. 气体分子的热运动越剧烈，气体温度就越低

C. 气体对器壁的压强是由大量气体分子对器壁不断碰撞而产生的

D. 当气体膨胀时，气体分子之间的势能减小，因而气体的内能减少

13. 在居室装修中经常使用到花岗岩、大理石等材料，这些材料都不同程度地含有放射性元素。比如，有一些含镭的材料会释放出放射性惰性气体氡，而氡产生后很快衰变成一系列放射性产物，最终成为稳定元素铅，这一过程会放出 α、β、γ 射线。根据有关放射性知识，下列说法中正确的是(　　)。
   A. 三种射线中，γ 射线的速度最大，穿透能力最强
   B. 三种射线中，α 粒子的质量最大，穿透能力最强
   C. 氡被吸入人体后，放射性衰变将会停止
   D. 随着气温的升高，氡的半衰期会变小
14. 下列说法中正确的是(　　)。
   A. 玛丽·居里首先提出了原子的核式结构模型
   B. 卢瑟福在 α 粒子散射实验中发现了电子
   C. 查德威克在 α 粒子散射实验中发现了中子
   D. 爱因斯坦为解释光电效应的实验规律提出了光子说
15. 如图所示为氢原子的能级示意图，一群氢原子处于 $n=3$ 的激发态，在向较低能级跃迁的过程中向外发出光子，用这些光照射逸出功为 2.49eV 的金属钠，下列说法中正确的是(　　)。

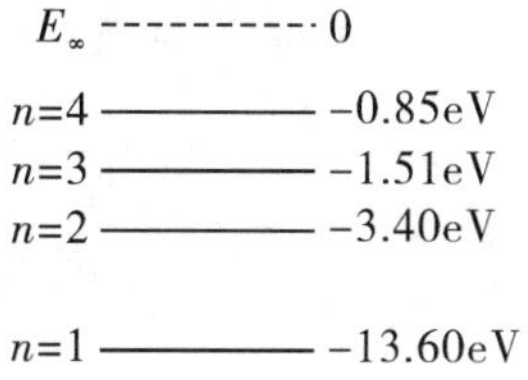

   A. 这群氢原子能发出三种频率不同的光，其中从 $n=3$ 跃迁到 $n=2$ 所发出的光波长最短
   B. 这群氢原子能发出两种频率不同的光，其中从 $n=3$ 跃迁到 $n=1$ 所发出的光频率最高
   C. 金属钠表面所发出的光电子的初动能最大值为 9.60eV
   D. 金属钠表面所发出的光电子的初动能最大值为 11.11eV

二、填空题（30 分。在答题卡相应的位置填入你认为正确的答案，每空 3 分）

16. 汽车以 20m/s 的速度做匀速直线运动，刹车后的加速度为 5m/s^2，那么开始刹车后 2s 的位移为________米。
17. 每秒做 100 次全振动的波源产生的波，以 10m/s 的速度传播，波长为________m。
18. 有 A、B 两个电容器，它们的电容分别是 C_1 和 C_2，并且 $C_1 > C_2$，那么，如果它们两极板间电势差相等，则电容器________所带的电荷多（填 A 或 B）。
19. $^{238}_{92}U$ 经过一系列的 α 衰变和 β 衰变后，最后变成稳定的 $^{206}_{82}Pb$，写出核反应的方程________________________________。
20. 某同学为验证机械能守恒定律设计了如下实验步骤：
   A. 用天平称出重物的质量；
   B. 把纸带固定到重物上，并把纸带穿过打点计时器，提升到一定高度；
   C. 拆掉导线，整理仪器；
   D. 断开电源，调整纸带，重做两次；

E. 用秒表测出重物下落的时间；

F. 用毫米刻度尺测出计数点与起点的距离，记录数据，并计算出结果，得出结论；

G. 把打点计时器接到低压交流电源上；

H. 接通电源，释放纸带；

I. 把打点计时器接到低压直流电源上；

J. 把打点计时器固定在桌边的铁架台上。

上述实验步骤中错误的是________，可有可无的是________，其余正确且必要的步骤按实验操作顺序排列是________________。（均只需填步骤的代号）

21. 为了测量两节串联干电池的电动势，某同学设计了如图甲所示的实验电路，其中 E 是待测电池组，内阻不能忽略；Ⓥ₁、Ⓥ₂是两只量程合适的相同的电表，内阻不是很大，且未知；S_1、S_2是单刀单掷开关；导线若干。

（1）请根据电路图甲，在图乙中将器材连成实物图。（3 分）

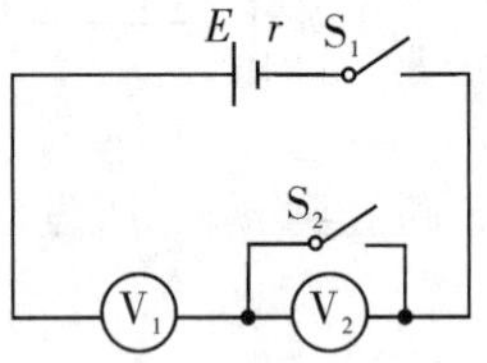

图甲

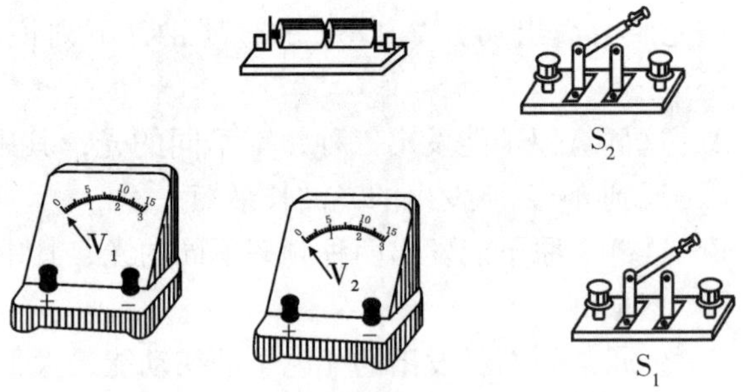

图乙

（2）实验需要测量的物理量是________________。

（3）用测出的物理量，推导出串联电池组电动势的表达式是________。

三、计算题（60 分。第 22 ~ 25 题必做，第 26 ~ 27 题选做一题）

22.（12 分）如图，位于水平地面上的质量为 M 的小木块，在大小为 F、方向与水平方向成 α 角的拉力作用下沿地面做匀速直线运动。求：

（1）地面对物体的支持力；

（2）木块与地面之间的滑动摩擦系数。

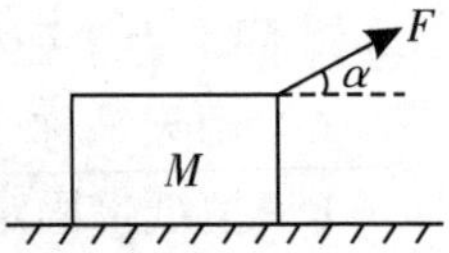

23. （12 分）某压力锅的结构如图所示。盖好密封锅盖，将压力阀套在出气孔上，给压力锅加热，当锅内气体压强达到一定值时，气体就把压力阀顶起。假定在压力阀被顶起时，停止加热。

（1）假定在一次放气过程中，锅内气体对压力阀及外界做功 1J，并向外界释放了 2J 的热量。锅内原有气体的内能如何变化？变化了多少？

（2）已知大气压强 p 随海拔高度 H 的变化满足 $p=p_0(1-aH)$，其中常数 $a>0$，结合气体定律分析在不同的海拔高度使用压力锅，当压力阀被顶起时锅内气体的温度有何不同。

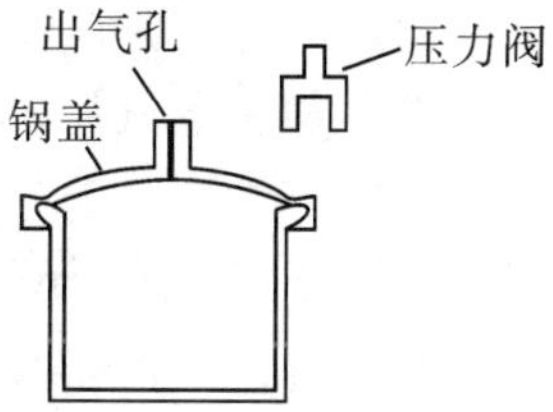

24. （12 分）如图所示，空间有与水平方向成 θ 角的匀强电场，一个质量为 m 的带电小球，用长为 L 的绝缘细线悬挂于 O 点。当小球静止时，细线恰好处于水平位置。现用一个外力将小球沿圆弧缓慢地拉到最低点，此过程小球的电荷量不变，则该外力做的功为多少？

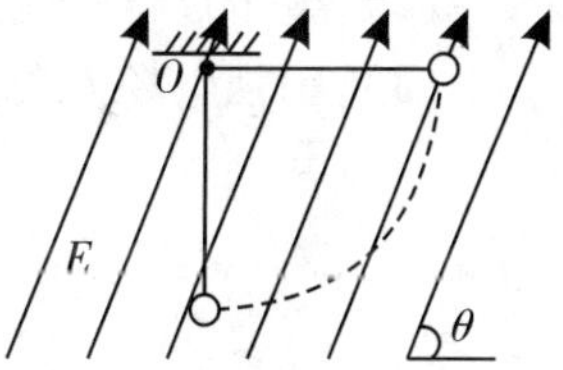

25. （12 分）某种液体的折射率为$\sqrt{2}$，在其液面下有一可绕水平轴 O 匀速转动的平面镜 OA，OA 的初始位置与液面平行，如图所示。在液面与平面镜间充满自左向右的平行光线，若在平面镜逆时针旋转一周的过程中，光线射入空气中的时间为 2s，试问：

（1）平面镜由初始位置转过多大角度时，光线开始进入空气？

（2）平面镜旋转的角速度是多大？

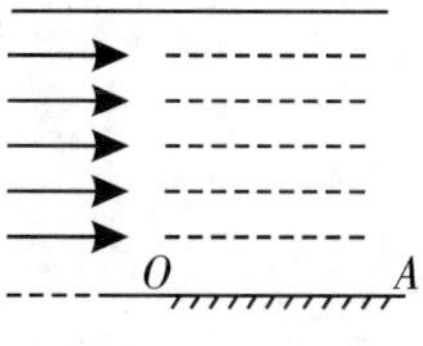

（以下第 26 ~ 27 题选做一题）

26. （12 分）弹射器是航母制造中的关键技术之一，重型喷气式战斗机在水平跑道上需要滑行 450m 以上才能达到起飞速度，而即使当今最大的“尼米兹”级航空母舰甲板的长度也不过 300 余米，依靠弹射器是重型战斗机在航母上起飞的必不可少的环节。

已知美军 F－14 战斗机重 3.0×10^7kg，在地面跑道上靠自身发动机提供动力需滑行 450m 才能到达 250km/h 的起飞速度，而这种战斗机在“尼米兹”号航母上，在蒸汽弹射器和自身发动机动力的共同作用下，可在 45m 内将速度增加到 250km/h。若F－14战斗机加速度滑行时，发动机动力和飞机受到的阻力都恒定，则“尼米兹”号上蒸汽弹射器使一架 F－14 战斗机起飞至少要做多少功？

27. （12 分）如图所示，某一质量为 m 的金属滑块，带电量大小为 q，以某一速度沿水平放置的木板进入电磁场空间，匀强磁场的方向垂直纸面向外，电场方向水平向右，滑块与木板之间的摩擦系数为 μ。已知滑块由 P 点沿木板做匀速直线运动到 Q 点与开关碰撞，将 Q 点的开关撞开，使电场消失，只保留磁场，离开开关时滑块的动能变为原来的 $\frac{1}{4}$，并匀速返回 P 处，设往复运动的总时间为 T，P、Q 间距离为 L，碰撞时间不计。求：

（1）磁感应强度 B 的大小；

（2）整个过程中克服摩擦力所做的功；

（3）匀强电场 E 的大小。

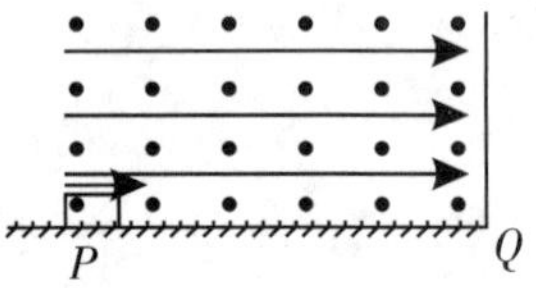

暨南大学、华侨大学联合招收港澳地区、台湾省、华侨、华人及其他外籍学生入学考试样题

物　理

答题卡

一、选择题

1 [A] [B] [C] [D]	6 [A] [B] [C] [D]	11 [A] [B] [C] [D]
2 [A] [B] [C] [D]	7 [A] [B] [C] [D]	12 [A] [B] [C] [D]
3 [A] [B] [C] [D]	8 [A] [B] [C] [D]	13 [A] [B] [C] [D]
4 [A] [B] [C] [D]	9 [A] [B] [C] [D]	14 [A] [B] [C] [D]
5 [A] [B] [C] [D]	10 [A] [B] [C] [D]	15 [A] [B] [C] [D]

以下为非选择题答题区，必须用黑色字迹的钢笔或签字笔在各题目的指定区域内作答，否则答案无效。

二、填空题

16. ____________　　17. ____________　　18. ____________

19. ____________________________

20. ____________　　____________　　____________

21. (1)

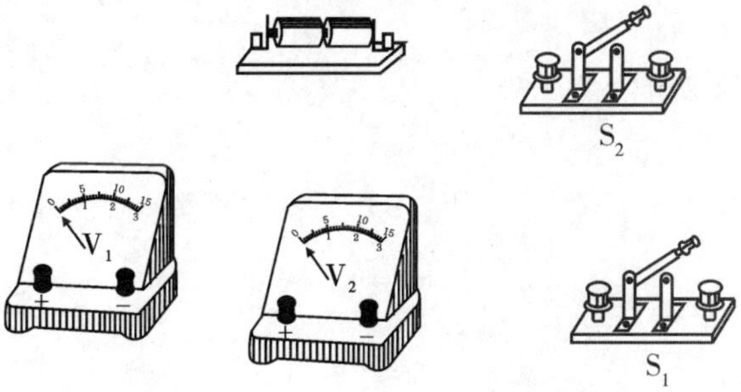

图乙

(2) ____

(3) ________________

三、计算题

22.
23.
24.

25.

第 26 ~ 27 题选做一题。

(　)

物理参考答案

一、选择题（60 分。以下各小题中只有一个答案是正确的，把你认为正确的答案分别填入答题卡中。每小题选对的给 4 分，多选、错选或不选的不给分）

1. C 2. A 3. D 4. B 5. B 6. A 7. B 8. C 9. C 10. D 11. B
12. C 13. A 14. D 15. C

二、填空题（30 分。在答题卡相应的位置填入你认为正确的答案，每空 3 分）

16. 30
17. 0.1
18. A
19. ${}^{238}_{92}U \rightarrow {}^{206}_{82}Pb + 8{}^{4}_{2}He + 6{}^{0}_{-1}e$
20. EI；A；JGBHDCF
21. （1）

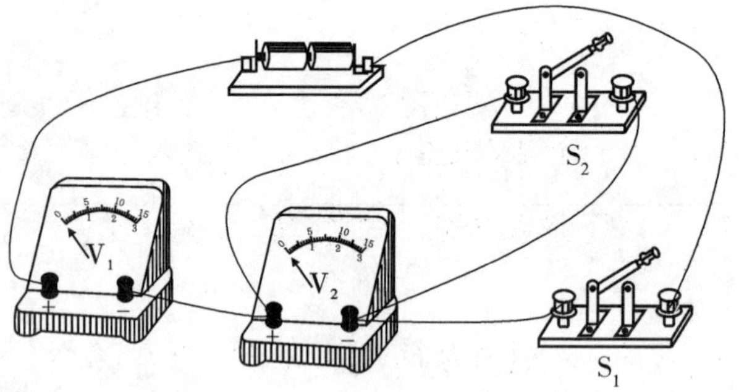

图乙

（2）闭合 S_1，读出 Ⓥ₁ 和 Ⓥ₂ 的读数 U；再闭合 S_2，读出 Ⓥ₁ 的读数 U'

（3）$E = \dfrac{U'U}{U' - U}$

三、计算题（60 分。第 22 ~ 25 题必做，第 26 ~ 27 题选做一题）

22. 解：（1）以物体为研究对象，由受力分析可知，竖直方向，N 为支持力

$Mg = N + F\sin\alpha$

所以 $N = Mg - F\sin\alpha$。

（2）水平方向，摩擦力 $f = \mu N = F\cos\alpha$

所以 $\mu = \dfrac{F\cos\alpha}{Mg - F\sin\alpha}$。

23. 解：（1）根据热力学第一定律有：

$\Delta E = W + Q = -1 - 2 = -3J$

故锅内气体内能减少，减少了 3J。

（2）由 $p=p_0(1-aH)$（其中 $a>0$）知，随着海拔高度的增加，大气压强减小；

由 $p_1=p+\frac{mg}{S}$ 知，随着海拔高度的增加，阀门被顶起时锅内气体压强减小；

根据查理定律 $\frac{p_1}{T_1}=\frac{p_2}{T_2}$ 可知，阀门被顶起时锅内气体温度随着海拔高度的增加而降低。

24. 解：由小球在平衡位置的受力可知：

$qE\cdot\sin\theta=mg$

设用外力缓慢拉至最低点外力做功为 W，由动能定理得：

$W+mgL-qE\cdot\sqrt{2}L\cdot\cos(\theta-45^\circ)=0$

解得 $W=mgL\cot\theta$。

25. 解：（1）设临界角为 C，则 $\sin C=\frac{1}{n}$，故 $C=45^\circ$。

由此可知当平面镜转过 $\alpha_1=22.5^\circ$ 时光线开始进入空气。

（2）当平面镜转过 67.5° 时，光线又发生全反射，不能进入空气，所以平面镜转过 $22.5^\circ\sim67.5^\circ$ 间光线进入空气。平面镜转动的角速度 $\omega=\frac{\alpha_2-\alpha_1}{t}=\frac{\pi}{8}$ rad/s。

26. 解：设 F－14 战斗机自身发动机的牵引力为 F，受到的阻力为 f，在水平地面跑道上起飞时，由动能定理有：

$(F-f)\cdot s_1=\frac{1}{2}mv^2-0$

在“尼米兹”号航母甲板上起飞时，有：

$W+Fs_2-fs_2=\frac{1}{2}mv^2$

代入数据，解得：弹射器至少需做的功 $W=6.5\times10^{10}$ J。

97

27. 解：（1）设开始时的速度为 v_0，离开开关时滑块的动能变为原来的 $\frac{1}{4}$，则 Q—P 过程的速度为 $\frac{v_0}{2}$，由滑块 P—Q—P 的过程，有：

$$\frac{L}{v_0}+\frac{L}{\frac{v_0}{2}}=T$$

解得 $v_0=\frac{3L}{T}$，

对滑块 Q—P 的过程，进行受力分析可知：

$$q\left(\frac{v_0}{2}\right)B = mg$$

$$B = \frac{2mg}{qv_0} = \frac{2mgT}{3qL}。$$

（2）经分析，只有 $P—Q$ 的过程，滑块受摩擦力。对滑块 $P—Q$ 的过程进行受力分析可知：

$f = \mu \cdot N = \mu(qv_0B + mg) = 3mg\mu$

$W_f = f \cdot s = 3\mu mgL$。

（3）由滑块 $P—Q$ 过程匀速运动，可知：

$qE = f$

$$E = \frac{f}{q} = \frac{3\mu mg}{q}。$$

化　学

考试要求

（1）正确理解化学基本概念、原理和定律等基础知识。
（2）掌握化学用语、数据、图表等表达化学知识的基本技能。
（3）认识化学现象的本质，理解化学变化的基本规律。
（4）掌握常见元素及其化合物的结构、性质、制法和用途。
（5）掌握有机化合物的结构、有机物分子中的官能团及其在物质中的作用；了解重要有机物的性质。
（6）能够正确使用化学实验中常用的仪器和药品；掌握实验的基本技能；了解实验研究的方法，能设计并完成一些化学实验；会处理简单的实验数据，并得出合理的解释。
（7）了解化学与生活、社会、环境及相关学科的联系。

考试范围与内容

一、基本概念

1．物质的组成和分类
元素、原子、分子、离子、单质（金属、非金属、稀有气体）、化合物（氧化物、氢化物、酸、碱及盐）、纯净物和混合物。

2．化学用语
元素符号、化学式（分子式）、电子式、结构式、结构简式、化学方程式。

3．化学中常用的量
阿伏伽德罗定律、质量守恒定律；相对原子质量、式量、物质的量、摩尔质量、气体摩尔体积；根据化学式计算式量及化合物中各种元素的质量比；根据化学方程式进行有关的计算。

二、原子结构和元素周期律

1．原子的组成
原子核、核外电子、质子、中子、核素、同位素；原子序数、核电荷数、质量数、质子数、中子数和电子数及它们之间的关系。

2. 原子核外电子排布

核外电子的运动特点、核外电子的排布规律，1 ~ 20 号元素的原子结构示意图。

3. 元素周期律

原子核外电子排布的周期性，原子半径、第一电离能、主要化合价等元素性质的周期性；同周期和同主族元素性质的递变规律（包括原子半径、主要化合价、金属性、非金属性、氧化性、还原性、最高价氧化物对应的水化物的酸碱性、氢化物的稳定性等）。

4. 元素周期表

元素周期表的结构、周期和族，元素周期表与原子结构的关系，元素的性质与原子结构的关系，1 ~ 20 号元素在周期表中的位置（周期、族）和主要性质。

5. 化学键和分子结构

化学键，离子键、共价键（极性键、非极性键和配位键）、金属键，用电子式表示典型离子键和共价键的形成过程；化学键的极性和分子的极性，分子间的作用力、氢键、分子晶体的特点；原子晶体、离子晶体和金属晶体的结构特点和主要性质。

三、分散系

1. 分散系

分散系的概念、分类，胶体的概念和主要性质。

2. 溶液及溶液的浓度

溶液的组成，饱和溶液、固体物质的溶解度及其有关计算；溶液的溶质质量分数、物质的量浓度、体积比浓度等的表示方法及有关计算。

四、化学反应速率与化学平衡

1. 化学反应与能量变化

化学反应的能量变化，燃烧热和中和热，热化学方程式的写法及表示的意义，有关反应热的简单计算。

2. 化学反应速率

化学反应速率的定性描述和简单计算；影响化学反应速率的因素，如浓度、压强、温度、催化剂等。

3. 化学平衡

可逆反应，化学平衡状态及特征；影响化学平衡的因素（浓度、温度、压强）；平衡移动原理（勒沙特列原理），运用化学反应速率与化学平衡原理讨论合成氨的适宜条件；计算反应物的转化率。

五、电解质溶液

1. 电解质

电解质和非电解质，强电解质和弱电解质，电解质的电离和电离方程式，弱电解质的电离平衡，离子反应和离子方程式。

2. 水的电离和溶液的 pH 值

水的电离、水的离子积常数，溶液的 pH 值；溶液的酸碱性与溶液的 pH 值的关系，有关 pH 值的计算。

3. 盐类水解

强酸弱碱盐和强碱弱酸盐的水解规律，溶液中离子的浓度、盐溶液的酸碱性的判断，影响盐类水解的主要因素，盐类水解在生产和生活中的应用。

六、氧化还原反应及电化学基础

1. 氧化还原反应

无机反应的基本类型（化合反应、分解反应、置换反应、复分解反应）；氧化还原反应的原理，氧化剂、还原剂、氧化性、还原性、氧化数、氧化反应、还原反应、氧化产物、还原产物等基本概念；重要的氧化剂和还原剂，用氧化数的变化进行氧化还原反应方程式的配平。

2. 电化学基础

原电池的原理、形成条件和电极反应式；金属腐蚀与防护方法；电解原理及其应用，离子的放电顺序、电极反应式和电解方程式，电解原理在氯碱工业、精炼铜、电镀中的应用。

七、元素化合物

1. 卤素

卤素原子结构的特点，卤素单质的性质及比较；氯气的性质、用途和制法；含氯化合物（氯酸钾、次氯酸及盐、漂白粉）的性质和用途；氯化氢和盐酸（氢氯酸）的性质；卤素离子的检验。

2. 其他非金属元素及其化合物

空气的组成，大气污染与环境保护；水资源与水的净化；氢气、氧气、氮气、硫、碳等非金属单质的结构、组成、性质和用途；过氧化氢、二氧化硫、硫化氢、氨气、氮氧化物（NO、NO_2）、碳氧化物（CO、CO_2）的性质；酸雨的形成、汽车尾气的成分；浓硫酸的特性，稀硫酸的性质，硝酸的氧化性和不稳定性；铵盐的性质及其检验，碳酸及盐的性质，碳酸的正盐与酸式盐之间的相互转化。

3. 碱金属

碱金属元素的原子结构与单质的性质及其变化规律；钠和钾的一些重要化合物（过氧化物、氢氧化物、盐）的性质和用途。

4. 其他重要的金属及其化合物

金属活动顺序表；镁、钙、铝在周期表中的位置及其性质和用途，氧化铝、氢氧化铝的性质（两性），明矾的性质和用途；铁在周期表中的位置，铁的性质和用途，二价铁的还原性和三价铁离子的氧化性，二价铁离子与三价铁离子之间的转化，二价铁离子与三价铁离子的检验方法；铜的性质和用途，铜的氧化物、氢氧化物及其盐的性质。

八、有机化学

1. 有机化合物

有机化合物的概念、结构特点和主要性质，同系物和同分异构体，含6个碳及以下的有机物的同分异构体的写法及IUPAC命名法；有机化合物的化学式和结构式的确定。

2. 有机化学反应的基本类型

取代反应（硝化、磺化、卤化），加成反应，加聚反应，缩聚反应，消去反应，酯化反应，水解反应，显色反应，氧化反应和还原反应。

3. 烃

甲烷、乙烯、乙炔和苯的分子结构、性质和用途，它们的同系物的分子组成通式、物理性质的变化规律、主要化学性质。

4. 烃的衍生物

官能团、卤代烃、醇、苯酚、醛（甲醛、乙醛）、羧酸（甲酸、乙酸、苯甲酸）、酯（乙酸乙酯）和油脂的分子组成及主要性质，烃、卤代烃、醇、醛、羧酸、酯等化合物之间的转化关系。

5. 糖类、蛋白质

糖类（葡萄糖、果糖、麦芽糖、蔗糖等）的分子组成和主要性质，蛋白质和氨基酸的基本结构和主要性质。

九、化学实验

1. 基本知识

化学实验常用仪器的名称和使用方法，常用试剂的存放和取用。

2. 物质的检验

常见气体：H_2、O_2、Cl_2、CO_2、SO_2、NH_3、HCl、CH_4、C_2H_4；

常见阳离子：H^+、Mg^{2+}、Ca^{2+}、Ba^{2+}、Al^{3+}、Fe^{2+}、Fe^{3+}、Cu^{2+}、NH_4^+；

常见阴离子：OH^-、Cl^-、Br^-、I^-、CO_3^{2-}、SO_4^{2-}、NO_3^-、SO_3^{2-}；

主要有机物：烯烃、炔烃、苯及苯的同系物，卤代烃，醇、醛、羧酸、葡萄糖、蛋白质。

3. 基本实验

粗盐的提纯，浓硫酸的稀释，一定溶质质量分数的溶液和一定物质的量浓度的溶液的配制，酸碱中和滴定的原理及方法，广泛pH试纸和酸碱指示剂（甲基橙、石蕊、酚酞）的使用。物质的制备，常见气体：H_2、O_2、Cl_2、CO_2、SO_2、NH_3、HCl、CH_4、C_2H_4的制备；有机物：乙烯、溴苯、乙酸乙酯的制备。

考试形式

考试采用闭卷、书面笔答的形式，考试时间为 120 分钟，试卷满分为 150 分。

试卷结构与题型

（1）各部分内容在试卷中所占的比例：
基本概念、原理和规律，约占 50%；元素化合物，约占 30%；有机化学，约占 20%。其中化学实验约占 20%，化学计算约占 20%。

（2）试卷设置的题型：

选择题	40%
填空题	约 10%
问答题	约 35%
计算题	约 15%

考生复习参考资料

1. 李志红，谢晓华．暨南大学、华侨大学联合招收港澳地区、台湾省、华侨、华人及其他外籍学生入学考试复习丛书·化学．广州：暨南大学出版社，2015.
2. 李志红，谢晓华．暨南大学、华侨大学两校联招及全国联招 2004—2011 化学试题详解丛书·化学．广州：暨南大学出版社，2013.
3. 李志红，谢晓华．暨南大学、华侨大学及全国联招考试模拟试题丛书·化学．广州：暨南大学出版社，2013.

样卷

暨南大学、华侨大学联合招收港澳地区、台湾省、华侨、华人及其他外籍学生入学考试样题

科目：化　学

答卷时间：120 分钟

本卷用到的相对原子质量： H－1，C－12，N－14，O－16，Na－23，S－32，Ba－137。

一、选择题（本题共 20 小题，每小题 3 分，共 60 分。下列每小题的 4 个选项中只有 1 个是正确的答案，请将正确答案的序号按题号填入答题卡中）

1. 邻苯二甲酸二丁酯（$C_{16}H_{22}O_4$）是一种常见的增塑剂，长期食用增塑剂超标的食品会对人体健康产生较大影响。它属于

A. 高分子化合物　B. 氧化物　C. 有机物　D. 无机物

2. 下列物质能使干燥的蓝色石蕊试纸变红又褪色的是

A. 氯气　B. 液氯　C. 氢氯酸　D. 氯水

3. 当光束通过下列分散系时，可观察到丁达尔效应的是

A. 乙醇溶液　B. 氯化钠溶液

C. 硫酸铜溶液　D. 氢氧化铁胶体

4. 下列物质中，碱性最强的是

A. $Fe(OH)_3$　B. NaOH　C. $Mg(OH)_2$　D. $Al(OH)_3$

5. ^{230}Th 和 ^{232}Th 是钍的两种同位素，^{232}Th 可以转化成 ^{233}U。下列有关 Th 的说法正确的是

A. ^{230}Th 和 ^{232}Th 的中子数相同　B. ^{232}Th 和 ^{233}U 的化学性质相同

C. ^{232}Th 转换成 ^{233}U 是化学变化　D. ^{230}Th 和 ^{232}Th 的化学性质相同

6. 在下列可逆反应中，增大压强或降低温度，均可使化学平衡向正反应方向移动的是

A. $2SO_2 + O_2 \rightleftharpoons 2SO_3(g)$，$\Delta H < 0$

B. $4NH_3 + 5O_2 \rightleftharpoons 4NO + 6H_2O(g)$，$\Delta H < 0$

C. $2NH_3 \rightleftharpoons N_2 + 3H_2$，$\Delta H > 0$

D. $SO_2 + NO_2 \rightleftharpoons SO_3(g) + NO$，$\Delta H < 0$

7. 用两支惰性电极插入下列溶液中，通电一段时间后，测得溶液的 pH 值不变（通电前后溶液的温度不变），则该溶液可能是

A. 稀 HCl 溶液　B. 稀 NaOH 溶液

C. 饱和 NaCl 溶液　D. 饱和 Na_2SO_4 溶液

8. 下列有关物质用途的说法，不正确的是

A. 晶体硅可用于制作半导体材料

B. 氢氧化铝可用于制胃酸中和剂

C. 氧化铝可用于制造耐高温的实验仪器

D. 氧化钠可用作呼吸面具中氧气的来源

9. 下列离子方程式中不正确的是

A. 澄清石灰水跟盐酸反应：$Ca(OH)_2 + 2H^+ = Ca^{2+} + 2H_2O$

B. 碘化钾溶液跟适量溴水反应：$2I^- + Br_2 = I_2 + 2Br^-$

C. 将金属钠加入水中：$2Na + 2H_2O = 2Na^+ + 2OH^- + H_2\uparrow$

D. 将氯气通入氯化亚铁溶液：$2Fe^{2+} + Cl_2 = 2Fe^{3+} + 2Cl^-$

10. 下列叙述中，指定粒子的数目约为 1mol 的是

A. 11.2L H_2中含有的氢原子数

B. 常温常压下，1.7g NH_3中含有的质子数

C. 标准状况下，22.4L H_2O 中含有的氧原子数

D. 1mol Na_2SO_4溶于水，所得溶液中含有的钠离子数

11. 下列反应不属于氧化还原反应的是

A. $CuO + H_2 \overset{\triangle}{=} Cu + H_2O$

B. $2C_2H_5OH + 2Na = 2C_2H_5ONa + H_2\uparrow$

C. $2HCl + FeS = FeCl_2 + H_2S\uparrow$

D. $2Fe^{3+} + Cu = Cu^{2+} + 2Fe^{2+}$

12. 向饱和澄清石灰水中加入少量 CaO，充分反应后，恢复到原来的温度，则所得溶液中

A. $c(Ca^{2+})$、$c(OH^-)$ 均增大　　B. $c(Ca^{2+})$、$c(OH^-)$ 均保持不变

C. $c(Ca^{2+})$、$c(OH^-)$ 均减小　　D. $c(OH^-)$ 增大、$c(H^+)$ 减小

13. 化学与日常生活密切相关，下列说法中错误的是

A. 碘酒是指单质碘的乙醇溶液　　B. 含碘盐是在食盐中添加碘单质

C. 氢氟酸可刻蚀石英制艺术品　　D. 装饰材料释放的甲醛会造成污染

14. 下列实验仪器中不宜直接用来加热的是

A. 试管　　B. 坩埚　　C. 蒸发皿　　D. 烧杯

15. 以下实验能获得成功的是

A. 用酸性 $KMnO_4$溶液鉴别乙烯和乙炔

B. 将铁屑、溴水、苯混合制溴苯

C. 实验室制乙烯用水浴加热

D. 铜丝烧热后立即伸入无水乙醇中，铜丝恢复原色，可得到乙醛

16. 相同质量的下列烃，在空气中充分燃烧需要氧气最多的是

A. C_2H_2　　B. C_3H_6　　C. C_4H_{10}　　D. C_6H_6

17. 下列有机物中，不属于糖类的是

A. 蔗糖　　B. 纤维素　　C. 氨基酸　　D. 淀粉

18. 分子式为C_8H_{10}的芳香烃，苯环上的一氯代物共有两种，该芳香烃的名称是

A. 对二甲苯　　B. 邻二甲苯　　C. 间二甲苯　　D. 乙苯

19. 现有3组混合物：①苯和水，②硝酸钾和氯化钠，③溴和溴化钠溶液，正确的分离方法依次是

A. 分液、萃取、蒸馏　　B. 萃取、盐析、分液

C. 分液、重结晶、萃取　　D. 蒸馏、过滤、分液

20. 下列有机物符合通式$C_nH_{2n-2}O_2$的是

A. 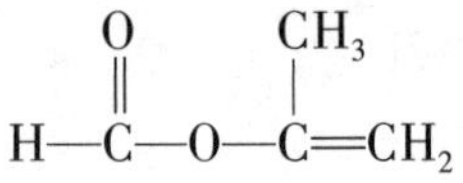　　B. 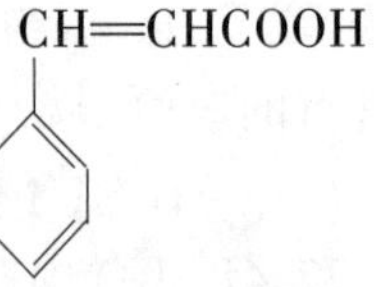

C. $CH_2=CH-CH=CHCOOH$　　D. $CH_3CH_2CH_2COOH$

二、填空题（本题共2小题，每空1分，共12分）

21. （6分）现有H、Fe、N、O、Na、C六种元素，选用合适的元素，按下列要求组成化合物（各举一例），写出各物质的化学式：

（1）难溶性碱________；（2）可溶性弱碱________；

（3）有色气体________；（4）弱酸________；

（5）水溶液呈碱性的盐________；（6）水溶液呈酸性的盐________。

22. （6分）现有四种有机物：A. $CH_2=CH_2$，B. $HCOOCH_2CH_3$，C. CH_3CH_2OH，D. CH_3COOH，请按下列要求填空（填字母）：

（1）能发生银镜反应的是________；（2）能发生消去反应的是________；

（3）能发生酯化反应的是________；（4）能与碳酸氢钠溶液反应的是________；

（5）能发生加聚反应的是________；（6）能发生水解反应的是________。

三、问答题（本题共5小题，共58分）

23. （8分）某温度时，在2.0L密闭容器内加入1.0mol SO_2和0.5mol O_2，发生如下反应，放出98.5kJ的热量：

$$2SO_2(g)+O_2(g) \rightleftharpoons 2SO_3(g)$$

请回答：

（1）写出该反应的热化学反应方程式________。

（2）反应进行2min后，测得SO_2为0.7mol，则2min内$v(SO_3)$ = ________mol/(L·min)。

（3）反应进行8min后达到了平衡，测得混合物的压强是开始时压强的0.75倍，则SO_2的平衡转化率是________；混合气体的平均分子量为________。

24. （10分）四种短周期元素在周期表中的相对位置如下所示，其中B元素原子最外层

电子数是电子层数的 3 倍。

A	B	
	C	D

请回答下列问题：

（1）C 在元素周期表中的位置是：________________________。

（2）写出 B 原子结构示意图：________________________。

（3）C 的氢化物与 B 的氢化物的稳定性强弱顺序为：________________。

（4）写出 A 的气态氢化物与 A 的最高价氧化物对应水化物反应的化学式及所含化学键的类型：____________________________________。

（5）写出 D 的最高价氧化物对应水化物的化学式：________________。

25.（14 分）如图是一套制取氨气并验证氨气性质的实验装置。

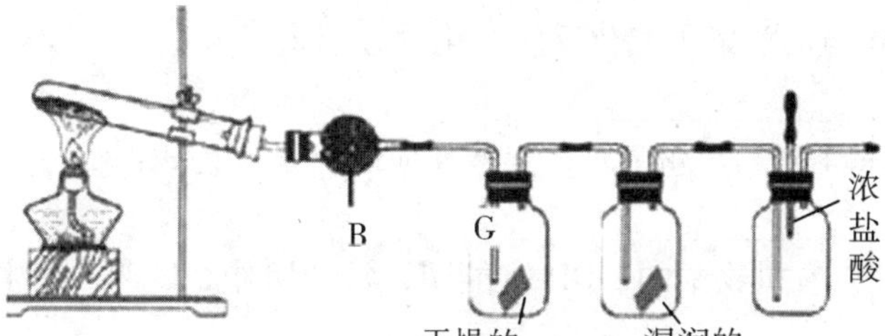

（1）A 中的化学反应方程式是______________________________________。

（2）B 中选择的试剂是______________，作用是____________________。

（3）C 装置中的现象是________________________________。

（4）当实验进行一段时间后，挤压 E 装置中的胶头滴管，滴入 1～2 滴浓盐酸，可观察到的现象是__________________。

（5）为防止过量氨气造成空气污染，需要在上述装置的末端增加一个__________。

（6）该装置在实验室还可以制取__________________气体。

26.（14 分）某固体混合物可能由 Na_2SO_4、$FeCl_3$、KI、KCl、$CaCl_2$ 和 Na_2CO_3 中的一种或几种组成。依次进行以下实验：

（1）混合物加水得无色透明溶液，可判断溶液中不含_______________。

（2）向上述溶液中滴加 $BaCl_2$ 溶液，有白色沉淀生成，初步判断溶液中可能含有____________。沉淀中滴加盐酸，沉淀不溶解，进一步确定溶液含____________，将该沉淀滤出，将滤液分成两份。

（3）将两份滤液中的一份，滴加氯水并加入 CCl_4，震荡后放置，CCl_4 层无色，可判断溶液中不含____________。

(4) 将另一份滤液中加入 $AgNO_3$ 溶液，有白色沉淀生成，该沉淀不溶于稀硝酸。初步判断溶液中可能含____________。

(5) 根据以上实验，可以判断混合物中肯定含有______________；上述实验还不能确定是否含有的是______________。

27. (12 分) 对羟基肉桂酸 (M) 是一种强效的导电材料，近年来在液晶显示器工业中研究广泛。其结构简式如图所示：

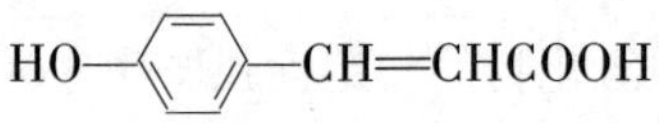

请回答：

(1) M 中含有官能团的名称是：______________。

(2) 写出 M 发生加聚反应生成的高分子化合物的结构简式：

________________________。

(3) 写出 M 与乙醇发生酯化反应的化学方程式：

________________________。

(4) 写出 1mol M 与足量 NaOH 溶液反应的化学方程式：

________________________。

(5) 为验证该有机物中的—OH 官能团，常选用什么试剂？产生怎样的实验现象？

__________________________；__________________________。

四、计算题（本题共 2 小题，每小题 10 分，共 20 分）

28. (10 分) 200mL 某浓度的盐酸与固态碳酸钠恰好完全反应，将生成的二氧化碳通过装有一定质量 Na_2O_2 的装置，设二氧化碳全部被吸收，这时装置内固体增重 11.2g。求：

(1) 参加反应的碳酸钠的质量；

(2) 盐酸的物质的量浓度。

29. (10 分) 在常温下，将 50mL pH = 1.0 的 $NaHSO_4$ 溶液与 50mL 0.1mol/L 的 $Ba(OH)_2$ 溶液相混合，充分反应后过滤。

(1) 写出该反应的化学方程式；

(2) 计算生成沉淀的质量；

(3) 计算反应后滤液的 pH 值。

暨南大学、华侨大学联合招收港澳地区、台湾省、华侨、华人及其他外籍学生入学考试样题

化　学

答题卡

一、选择题

1 [A] [B] [C] [D]	6 [A] [B] [C] [D]	11 [A] [B] [C] [D]	16 [A] [B] [C] [D]
2 [A] [B] [C] [D]	7 [A] [B] [C] [D]	12 [A] [B] [C] [D]	17 [A] [B] [C] [D]
3 [A] [B] [C] [D]	8 [A] [B] [C] [D]	13 [A] [B] [C] [D]	18 [A] [B] [C] [D]
4 [A] [B] [C] [D]	9 [A] [B] [C] [D]	14 [A] [B] [C] [D]	19 [A] [B] [C] [D]
5 [A] [B] [C] [D]	10 [A] [B] [C] [D]	15 [A] [B] [C] [D]	20 [A] [B] [C] [D]

以下为非选择题答题区，必须用黑色字迹的钢笔或签字笔在指定的黑色框区域内作答，否则答案无效。

二、填空题

21.（6 分）

（1）__________　（2）__________　（3）__________

（4）__________　（5）__________　（6）__________

22.（6 分）

（1）__________　（2）__________　（3）__________

（4）__________　（5）__________　（6）__________

三、问答题

23.（8 分）

（1）______________________________

（2）____________

（3）____________　______________

24.（10 分）

（1）____________　（2）____________　（3）____________

（4）______________________________

（5）______________________________

25．（14 分） （1）________________ （2）________　________ （3）________　（4）________ （5）________________ （6）________
26．（14 分） （1）________ （2）________　________ （3）________ （4）________ （5）________　________
27．（12 分） （1）________ （2）________ （3）________________ （4）________________ （5）________　________

四、计算题

28．（10 分）
29．（10 分）

化学参考答案

一、选择题（本题共20小题，每小题3分，共60分）

1. C 2. D 3. D 4. B 5. D 6. A 7. D 8. D 9. A 10. B

11. C 12. B 13. B 14. D 15. D 16. C 17. C 18. B 19. C 20. A

二、填空题（本题共2小题，每空1分，共12分）

21. （1）$Fe(OH)_2$或$Fe(OH)_3$

（2）$NH_3 \cdot H_2O$

（3）NO_2

（4）H_2CO_3或CH_3COOH

（5）Na_2CO_3或$NaHCO_3$或CH_3COONa

（6）$Fe(NO_3)_2$或$Fe(NO_3)_3$或NH_4NO_3

22. （1）B （2）C （3）CD （4）D （5）A （6）B

三、问答题（本题共5小题，共58分）

23. （1）$SO_2(g) + 1/2O_2(g) \overset{\triangle}{\rightleftharpoons} SO_3(g)$ $\Delta H = -98.5kJ/mol$

（2）0.075

（3）75% 71.1

24. （1）第三周期，VIA

（2）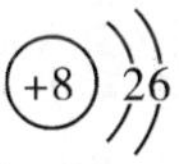

（3）$H_2O > H_2S$

（4）NH_4NO_3，离子键、共价键、配位键

（5）$HClO_4$

25. （1）$2NH_4Cl + Ca(OH)_2 \overset{\triangle}{=\!=} 2NH_3\uparrow + 2H_2O + CaCl_2$

（2）碱石灰 干燥NH_3中的水蒸气，以防对后面的实验产生影响

（3）无现象

（4）冒白烟

（5）装有水或稀盐酸的尾气处理瓶（防倒吸）

（6）O_2和CH_4

26. （1）$FeCl_3$

（2）Na_2SO_4，Na_2CO_3 Na_2SO_4

（3）KI

（4）Cl^-

（5）Na_2SO_4　KCl

27.（1）酚羟基、碳碳双键、羧基

（2）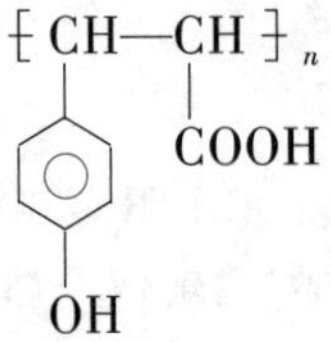

（3）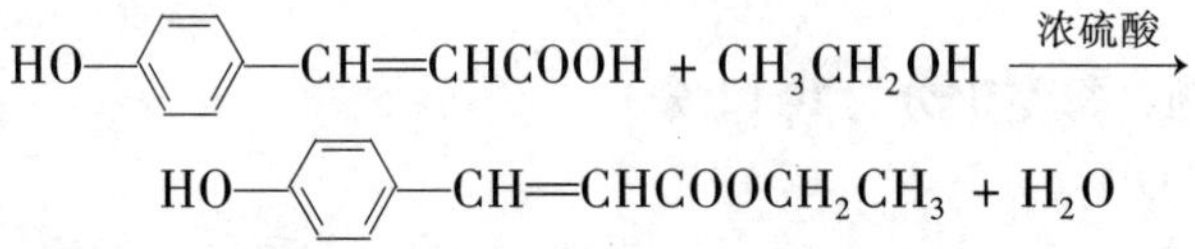

（4）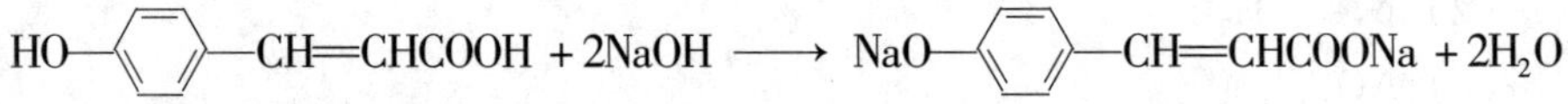

（5）$FeCl_3$　溶液呈紫色

四、计算题（本题共 2 小题，每小题 10 分，共 20 分）

28.（1）42.4g　（2）4mol/L

29.（1）$Ba(OH)_2 + NaHSO_4 = BaSO_4 \downarrow + NaOH + H_2O$

（2）1.165g　（3）pH = 12.7

生　物

考试要求

1. 理解能力

（1）能理解所学知识的要点，把握知识间的内在联系，形成知识的网络结构。

（2）能用文字、图表以及数学等多种表达形式准确地描述生物学方面的内容。

（3）能运用所学知识与观点，通过比较、分析与综合等方法对某些生物学问题进行解释、推理，作出合理的判断或得出正确的结论。

2. 实验与探究能力

（1）能独立完成课程所列的生物实验，包括理解实验目的、原理、方法和操作步骤，掌握相关的操作技能，并能将这些实验涉及的方法和技能进行综合运用。

（2）具备验证简单生物学事实的能力，并能对实验现象和结果进行解释、分析和处理。

（3）具有对一些生物学问题进行初步探究的能力，包括运用观察、实验与调查，假说演绎，建立模型与系统分析等科学研究方法。

（4）能对一些简单的实验方案作出恰当的评价和修订。

3. 获取信息的能力

（1）能从课外材料中获取相关的生物学信息，并能运用这些信息，结合所学知识解决相关的生物学问题。

（2）关注对科学、技术和社会发展有重大影响和意义的生物学新进展以及生物科学发展史上的重要事件。

4. 综合运用能力

理论联系实际，综合运用所学知识解决自然界和社会生活中的一些生物学问题。

考试范围与内容

根据普通高等学校对新生文化素质的要求，依据《暨南大学、华侨大学联合招收港澳地区、台湾省、华侨、华人及其他外籍学生入学考试复习大纲（2016—2020）》，以及与大纲配套的《暨南大学、华侨大学联合招收港澳地区、台湾省、华侨、华人及其他外籍学生入学考试复习丛书·生物》的内容来确定生物学科的考试内容。《暨南大学、华侨大学联合招收港澳地区、台湾省、华侨、华人及其他外籍学生考试复习丛书·生物》参考了内地新课标生物的教学内容和香港改学制后的中学生物学教学内容，选择了生物科学的核心内容，同时也是现代生物科学发展最迅速、成果应用最广泛、与社会和个人生活关系最密切的领域。所选内容能够帮助学生从微观和宏观两个方面认识生命系统的物质和结构基础、发展和变化规律以及生命系统中各组分间的相互作用。因此，所选内容对于提高学生的生物科学素养具有不可或缺的作用。书中的阅读资料是为了帮助学生更好地理解课文的有关内容，为了满足学生多样化发展的需要而设计的，有助于拓展学生的生物科技视野，增进学生对生物科技与社会关系的理解，提高学生的实践能力和探究能力。阅读资料内容不在考试内容之列。生物学科命题要体现生物课程属于科学课程的性质。重视对考生科学素养的考查，在生物科学和技术的基础知识、科学探究的方法、获取新知识和处理信息的能力、思维能力、分析和解决实际问题的能力等方面对考生的表现进行测量。重视理论联系实际，关注科学技术、社会经济和生态环境的协调发展。

具体内容如下：

一、细胞与生命分子

1. 生命的分子组成：组成生物体的化学元素；组成生物体的化合物。
2. 细胞的结构：细胞的发现和细胞学说的建立；细胞的形状和大小；真核细胞的亚显微结构及功能；细胞的生物膜系统；原核细胞的结构。
3. 细胞的代谢：酶与生物催化剂；ATP——细胞的能量“通货”；光合作用；细胞呼吸；新陈代谢的基本类型。
4. 细胞的分裂：有丝分裂；无丝分裂；减数分裂。
5. 细胞的分化、衰老、凋亡和癌变：细胞的分化；细胞的衰老；细胞的凋亡；细胞的癌变；细胞分裂、细胞分化和细胞癌变的区别。

二、遗传和变异

1. 分子遗传学：DNA是主要的遗传物质；DNA分子的结构和复制；基因的表达；基因工程。
2. 遗传的基本定律：基因的分离定律；基因的自由组合定律；性别决定和伴性遗传。
3. 人类遗传病：人类遗传病的种类；遗传病的治疗方法；优生学。
4. 生物的变异：基因突变；基因重组；染色体变异。
5. 生物的进化：自然选择学说及其发展；现代生物进化理论简介；生物的进化过程和分界。

三、生物与环境

1. 生态因素：生态因素对生物的影响；生物对环境的适应与影响。
2. 种群和生物群落：种群；生物群落。
3. 生态系统：生态系统的类型；生态系统的结构；生态系统的能量流动；生态系统的物质循环。

4．生态环境的保护：生物圈的概念；生物圈稳态的自我维持；人类活动对生物圈的影响；生物圈的保护和人类社会的可持续发展；环境污染对生物的不利影响；生物多样性保护的意义和措施。

四、人体生命活动的调节和免疫

1．人的营养和物质的运输：人体的营养作用；人体的运输作用。
2．人体内环境的控制及健康：内稳态及维持；水和无机盐的平衡和调节；血糖的调节；体温调节；含氮废物和人类的排泄系统。
3．免疫：传染病；免疫系统的组成；免疫机制；免疫失调引起的疾病。

五、微生物

1．各类微生物：细菌；病毒；真菌。
2．微生物的营养和生长：微生物的营养和生长；发酵工程简介。

六、实验

【实验一】生物组织中可溶性糖、脂肪、蛋白质的鉴定。
【实验二】探索影响淀粉酶活性的条件（选做）。
【实验三】叶绿体中色素的提取和分离。
【实验四】观察植物细胞的有丝分裂。
【实验五】观察 DNA 和 RNA 在细胞中的分布。
【实验六】ABO 血型鉴定及交叉配血实验。

七、阅读资料

与蛋白质相关的计算；膜泡运输的基本概念；线粒体 DNA 的重要作用；线粒体和叶绿体结构和生理功能的比较；细胞器分类归纳；兼性厌氧型生物——酵母菌；光合作用与呼吸作用的关系；细胞不能无限长大；细胞工程；与 DNA 碱基数量有关的计算方法；与 DNA 分子复制有关的计算方法；基因；遗传密码的特点；基因工程的延伸——蛋白质工程；DNA 重组技术的基本工具；基因工程的基本操作程序；基因工程的应用；与遗传定律有关的基本概念汇总；基因的分离定律和基因的自由组合定律的区别和联系；自由组合定律的细胞学基础；生物的性别决定；色盲症的发现；伴性遗传的特点；人类基因组计划；生物变异的种类；三种可遗传变异的比较；哈迪—温伯格定律（Hardy－Weinberg equilibrium）；人种漫谈；非生物因素对生物的影响；保护色、警戒色和拟态的辨析；种群密度的一种调查方法——标志重捕法；解读三大营养物质代谢；狂犬病简介；埃博拉病毒；非典型肺炎。

考试形式

考试采用闭卷、书面笔答的形式，考试时间为 120 分钟，试卷满分为 150 分。

试卷结构与题型

试卷分为三部分，第一部分为选择题，每小题答案唯一，本大题共 30 小题，每小题 2 分，共 60 分；第二部分为判断题，本大题共 10 小题，每小题 2 分，共 20 分；第三部分为简答题，共 70 分。试题难度：试卷包括容易题、中等难度题和难题三种类型，以中等难度题为主。

考生复习参考资料

1. 何红卫. 暨南大学、华侨大学联合招收港澳地区、台湾省、华侨、华人及其他外籍学生入学考试复习丛书・生物. 广州：暨南大学出版社，2015.
2. 何红卫. 暨南大学、华侨大学两校联招及全国联招 2004—2011 年试题详解丛书・生物. 广州：暨南大学出版社，2013.
3. 何红卫. 暨南大学、华侨大学及全国联招考试模拟试题丛书・生物. 广州：暨南大学出版社，2013.

样卷

暨南大学、华侨大学联合招收港澳地区、台湾省、华侨、华人及其他外籍学生入学考试样题

科目：生　物

答卷时间：120 分钟

一、选择题（本大题共 30 小题，每小题 2 分，共 60 分。每小题给出的四个选项中，只有一个选项最符合题目要求。请将正确答案按题号填涂在答题卡上）

1. 临床通过检测尿液中一定时间内的含“N”量，可以粗略地估算下列哪一物质在该时间内的氧化分解量

A. 蛋白质（protein）　　B. 脂肪（fat）

C. 葡萄糖（glucose）　　D. 淀粉（starch）

2. 下列关于蛋白质（protein）和酶（enzyme）的叙述，错误的一项是

A. 蛋白质的结构多样性决定其功能多样性

B. 胃蛋白酶（pepsin）的基本单位是氨基酸（amino acid）

C. 肽酶（peptidase）能使蛋白质分解为多肽（polypeptide）

D. 相同种类、数目的氨基酸组成的蛋白质可能不同

3. 与植物细胞比较，细菌的细胞结构中所没有的是

A. 细胞壁　　B. 细胞膜

C. 成形的细胞核　　D. 细胞质

4. 下列哪个细胞器（organelle）无膜结构

A. 叶绿体（chloroplast）

B. 线粒体（mitochondrion）

C. 核糖体（ribosome）

D. 高尔基体（Golgibody）

5. 胃液的蛋白酶（protease）在小肠中会失去活性，此种现象是与酶（enzyme）的何种特性有关

A. 酶具有专一性（specificity）

B. 酶无法重复使用

C. 酶活性受到温度的影响

D. 酶活性受 pH 值影响

6. 能够促使唾液淀粉酶水解的酶是

A. 淀粉酶（amylase）　　B. 蛋白酶（protease）

C. 脂肪酶（lipase）　　D. 麦芽糖酶（maltase）

7. 下列图中，表示细胞有丝分裂过程中，核内 DNA 含量变化的是

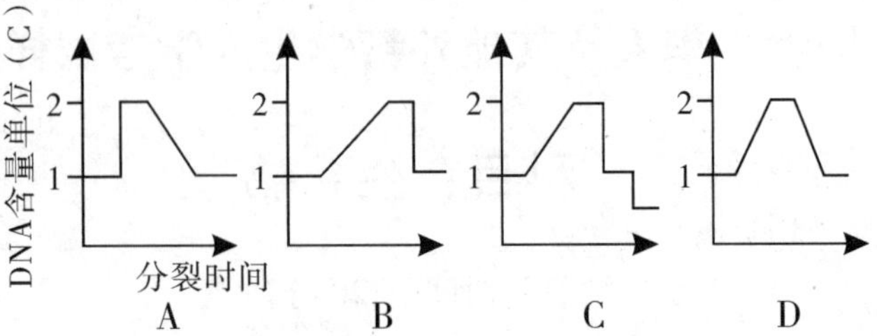

8. 噬菌体（bacteriophage）侵染细菌的实验是说明 DNA 是遗传物质的有力证据之一。下列叙述中属于该实验不能证实的是

A. DNA 能够进行自我复制　　B. DNA 能控制蛋白质的合成

C. DNA 能产生可遗传的变异　　D. DNA 能控制噬菌体的性状遗传

9. 下列属于有丝分裂（mitosis）和减数分裂（meiosis）过程中出现的共同点是

A. 同源染色体（homologous chromosome）的联会

B. 同源染色体的分离

C. 着丝点（kinetochore）分裂，姐妹染色单体（sister chromatid）分开

D. 子细胞染色体数目是母细胞的一半

10. 下图为处于不同分裂时期的某生物的细胞示意图，下列叙述中正确的是

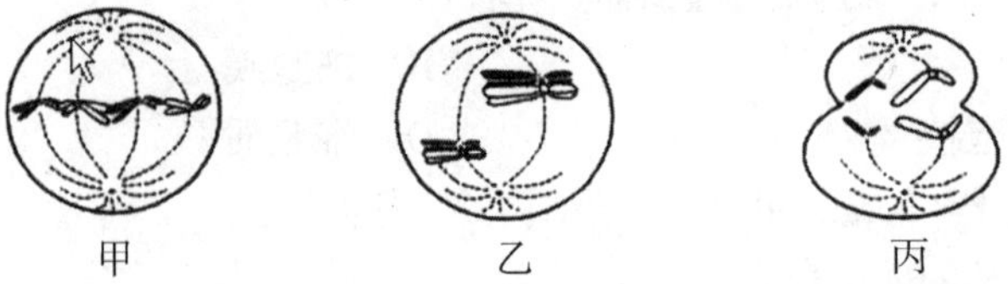

A. 甲、乙、丙中都有同源染色体　　B. 卵巢中可能同时出现这三种细胞

C. 能够出现基因重组的是甲、乙　　D. 丙的子细胞是精细胞

11. 科学家将含人的 α－抗胰蛋白酶基因的 DNA 片段，注射到羊的受精卵（zygote）中，该受精卵发育的羊能分泌含 α－抗胰蛋白酶的奶。这一过程不涉及

A. DNA 按照碱基互补配对原则（the principle of complementary base pairing）自我复制

B. DNA 以其一条链为模板合成 RNA

C. RNA 以自身为模板自我复制

D. 按照 RNA 密码子的排列顺序合成蛋白质（protein）

12. 由 n 个碱基组成的基因，控制合成由 1 条多肽链组成的蛋白质（protein）。氨基酸（amino acid）的平均分子量为 a，则该蛋白质的分子量最大为

A. $\frac{na}{6}$　　B. $\frac{na}{3}-18\ (\frac{n}{3}-1)$

C. $na-18\ (n-1)$　　D. $\frac{na}{6}-18\ (\frac{n}{6}-1)$

13. 下列有关光合作用（photosynthesis）暗反应（dark reaction）的表述，正确的是
A. 暗反应在细胞质基质中进行
B. 暗反应的产物只有糖类物质
C. 自然状态下，光照会影响暗反应的进行
D. 暗反应的本质是实现了无机物向储能的有机物的转化

14. 人红细胞的渗透压与 x 浓度的食盐水相当，而浸在 y 浓度食盐水中的红细胞破裂；浸在 z 浓度食盐水中的红细胞收缩，则这三种食盐水的浓度大小依次为
A. $x>y>z$　B. $y>z>x$　C. $z>y>x$　D. $z>x>y$

15. 已知一对夫妇生有一个 O 型血的男孩和一个 AB 型血的女孩。这对夫妇再生一个孩子，与该男孩的血型（blood type）相同的概率是
A. 1/16　B. 1/8　C. 1/4　D. 1/2

16. 一对表现型（phenotype）正常的夫妇，他们的母亲都是白化病（albinism），那么这对夫妇生一个正常男孩的概率是
A. 1/8　B. 1/16　C. 3/8　D. 3/16

17. 某遗传病是常染色体（autosome）隐性遗传，我们可以预期的是
A. 如果某个孩子是患者，这个孩子的祖父也是患者
B. 两个患者可生下患病男孩，但不能生下患病女孩
C. 两个患者不可能有一个正常的孩子
D. 患者和非患者所生的孩子都是正常的

18. 在下图的四个种群分布类型中，哪一类型种群灭绝的可能性最大？

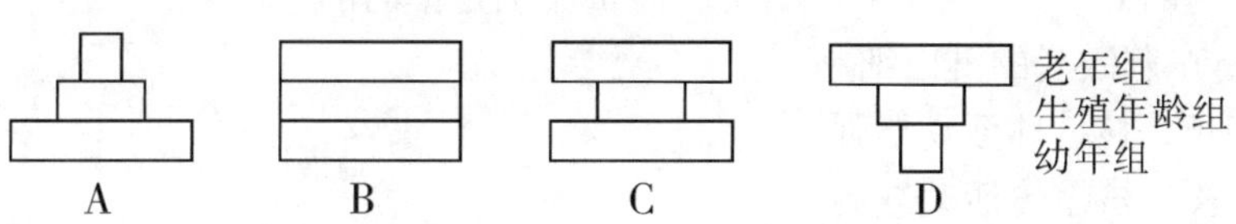

19. 下列各组生物之间，对于食物竞争（competition）最激烈的是
A. 蛙与昆虫　B. 狼和兔　C. 牛和羊　D. 鲸和磷虾

20. 在生物的生命活动中，能产生 ATP 的细胞结构有
A. 细胞核（nucleus）、高尔基体（Golgibody）、叶绿体（chloroplast）
B. 线粒体（mitochondrion）、高尔基体（Golgibody）、细胞质基质
C. 细胞质基质、线粒体、叶绿体
D. 细胞核、线粒体、核糖体（ribosome）

21. 如果 DNA 分子模板链上的 TAA 变成了 TAC，那么相应的遗传密码将会

A．由 AUU 变为 AUG　　B．由 UUA 变为 UAC
C．由 AUG 变为 AUU　　D．由 UAA 变为 UAC

22．与有丝分裂（mitosis）相比较，只发生在减数分裂（meiosis）过程的是
①染色体（chromosome）复制　②同源染色体（homologous chromosome）配对　③细胞（cell）数目增多　④基因重组　⑤基因分离　⑥着丝点（kinetochore）分裂
A．②④⑤　B．②③④　C．④⑤　D．②④

23．下列何种维生素（vitamin）与钙质的吸收有关
A．维生素 A　　B．维生素 D
C．维生素 E　　D．维生素 K

24．由于天气寒冷，同学们将门窗紧闭，在这密闭的教室里，时间一长就会出现头晕，注意力不能集中，记忆力下降，引起这些现象的下列原因中不正确的是
A．低血糖使脑细胞葡萄糖供应不足
B．脑部缺氧
C．线粒体（mitochondrion）不能产生足量的 ATP
D．脑细胞能量供应不足

25．人在发高烧时食欲降低，感觉食之无味，其原因是
A．体温升高，破坏了体温调节系统，从而影响了肠胃的吸收
B．体温升高，导致肠胃不能及时排空
C．体温升高，完全抑制了消化酶的分泌
D．体温升高，消化酶的活性受到影响

26．一条食物链中，兔子不会吃狼，但狼可以吃兔子，该食物链的不可逆性说明在一个生态系统中
A．水循环是单向的　　B．氧循环是单向的
C．碳循环是单向的　　D．能量流动是单向的

27．受抗原（antigen）刺激后的淋巴细胞
A．细胞周期变长，核糖体活动增强
B．细胞周期变长，核糖体活动减弱
C．细胞周期变短，核糖体活动减弱
D．细胞周期变短，核糖体活动增强

28．某学生在玻璃温室里进行植物栽培实验。为此，他对室内空气中的 CO_2 含量进行了24小时的测定，下图所示曲线中能正确表示其测定结果的是（横坐标为当日时间，纵坐标为 CO_2 浓度）

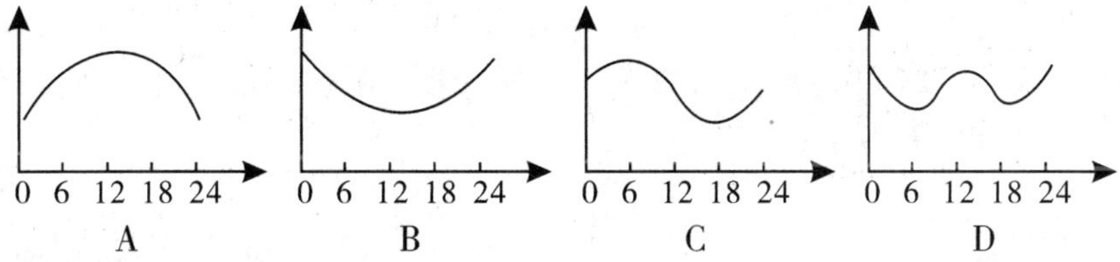

29. 下列营养物质中，人体需要量小，但对人体生理活动作用很大的物质是
    A. 糖类（carbohydrate）　　B. 蛋白质（protein）
    C. 脂类（lipid）　　D. 维生素（vitamin）
30. 医生给低血糖休克病人静脉注射5%葡萄糖液，其主要目的是
    A. 供给全面营养
    B. 供给能源物质
    C. 维持细胞的渗透压（osmotic pressure）
    D. 供给水分

二、判断题（对的画“T”，错的画“F”。本大题共 10 **小题，每小题** 2 **分，共** 20 **分。请将正确答案按题号填涂在答题卡上）**

31. 染色质和染色体是同一物质在细胞的不同时期的不同表现形式。
32. 有氧呼吸（aerobic respiration）和无氧呼吸（anaerobic respiration）是两个完全不同的过程。
33. 细胞有丝分裂（mitosis）周期包括前期、中期、后期和末期。
34. 女孩是色盲（achromatopsia）基因携带者，则该色盲基因是由父方遗传来的。
35. 物质出入细胞，有膜上载体参加时，一定耗能。
36. DNA 是由多个包括鸟嘌呤（G）、胞嘧啶（C）、腺嘌呤（A）和脲嘧啶（U）等核苷酸小分子所聚合而成的大分子。
37. 草食性动物不如肉食性动物凶猛，总是有相当一部分草食性动物被肉食性动物吃掉，所以生态系统中，必定是肉食性动物要多于草食性动物。
38. 与酶一样，转运 RNA 也具有专一性，在蛋白质（protein）的翻译过程中，只能运载一种特定的氨基酸（amino acid）。
39. 在双链 DNA 分子中，碱基的比率总是$\frac{A+G}{T+C}=1$。
40. 菟丝子是一种缺乏叶绿素的植物，但可通过吸取其他植物的营养汁液维生，故在生态系统中菟丝子扮演消费者（consumer）的角色。

三、简答题（共 70 **分）**

41. （6 分）香蕉果实成熟过程中，果实中的贮藏物不断代谢转化，香蕉逐渐变甜。图 A 中 I、II 两条曲线分别表示香蕉果实成熟过程中两种物质含量的变化趋势，请回

答：取成熟到第 X 天和第 Y 天的等量香蕉果肉，分别加等量的蒸馏水制成提取液，然后在 a、b 试管中各加 5mL 第 X 天的提取液，在 c、d 试管中各加 5mL 第 Y 天的提取液，如图 B 所示：

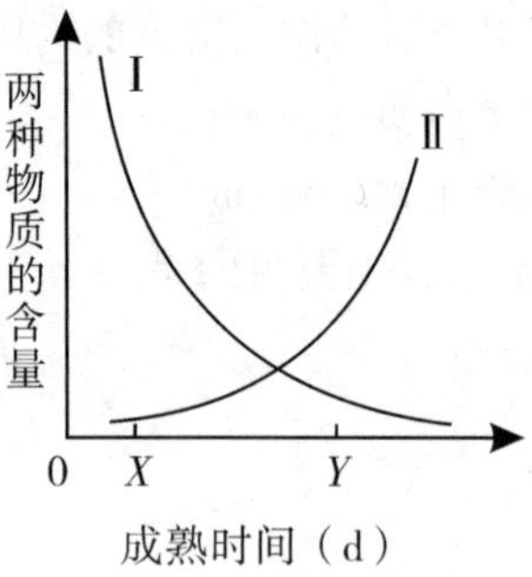

图A

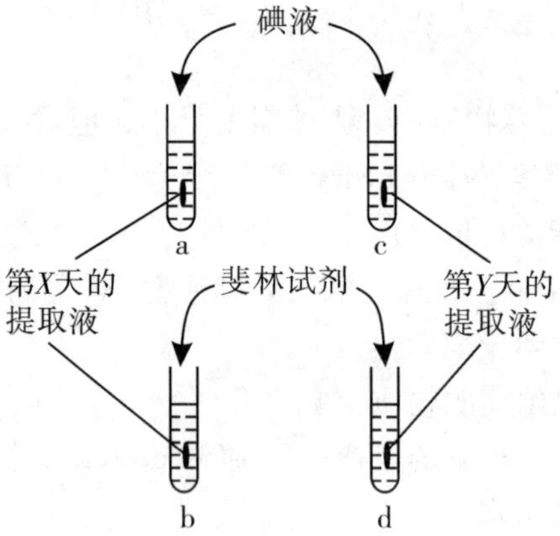

图B

（1）在 a、c 试管中各加入等量碘液后，a 管呈蓝色，与 a 管相比 c 管的颜色更浅，两管中被检测的物质是________，图 A 中表示这种物质含量变化趋势的曲线是________。

（2）在 b、d 试管中加入等量的斐林试剂，煮沸后，b 管呈砖红色，与 b 管相比 d 管的颜色更深，两管中被检测的物质是________，图 A 中表示这种物质含量变化趋势的曲线是________。

（3）已知乙烯利能增加细胞内乙烯的含量，促进香蕉成熟，如果在第 X 天喷施乙烯利，从第 X 天开始，曲线 I 将呈现出________（加快、减慢）下降的趋势，曲线 II 将呈现出________（加快、减慢）上升的趋势。

42.（9 分）将下列细胞结构与其功能对应起来。

①细胞膜（cell membrane）	A 光合作用场所
②叶绿体（chloroplast）	B 蛋白质合成场所
③线粒体（mitochondrion）	C 控制细胞渗透压
④核糖体（ribosome）	D 细胞的控制中心
⑤内质网（endoplasmic reticulum）	E 控制物质进出细胞
⑥液泡（vacuole）	F 有氧呼吸场所
⑦中心体（centrosome）	G 有机物加工运输场所
⑧细胞核（nucleus）	H 参与动物细胞有丝分裂
⑨高尔基体（Golgibody）	I 加工糖类或蛋白质

43.（12 分）下图为 3 个不同时期的细胞分裂模式图，请依图回答：

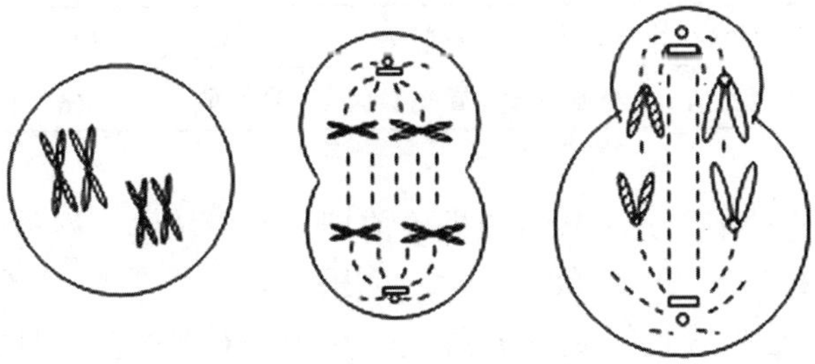

A　　　　B　　　　C

（1）图 A 属________分裂的________期，细胞中有________条染色单体。

（2）图 B 处于________分裂的__________期，此细胞的名称是 ______，其分裂后的子细胞叫________。

（3）图 C 处于________期，细胞名称为____________，它分裂后得到的子细胞是________。

（4）A、C 两图中染色体数之比为________，DNA 分子数之比为________。

44.（10 分）中心法则揭示了生物遗传信息由 DNA 向蛋白质传递与表达的过程。请回答下列问题。

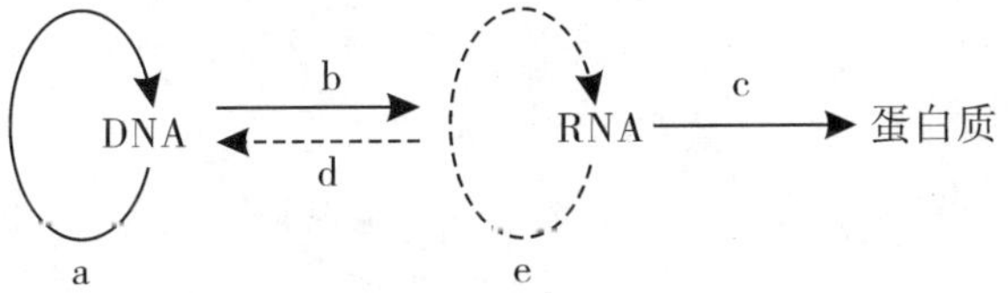

（1）a、b、c、d 所表示的四个过程依次分别是________、________、________和________。

（2）需要 tRNA 和核糖体同时参与的过程是__________（用图中的字母回答）。

（3）真核细胞基因突变发生的时期是图中__________过程中。

（4）在真核细胞中，a 和 b 两个过程发生的主要场所是____________。

（5）能特异性识别信使 RNA 上密码子的物质是__________，后者所携带的物质是__________。

（6）正常人体内的遗传信息传递与表达的途径是________________（用图中的字母回答）。

45.（6 分）细胞分裂间期是 DNA 复制和蛋白质合成等物质积累的过程。

（1）在 DNA 的复制过程中，DNA 在________的作用下，双螺旋链解开成为两条单链，并以每一条单链为模板，采用________复制方式合成子代 DNA 分子。

（2）某基因中的一段序列为……TAT GAG CTC GAG TAT……据下表提供的遗传密

码推测其编码的氨基酸序列：______________________。

密码子	CAC	UAU	AUA	CUC	GUG	UCC	GAG
氨基酸	组氨酸	酪氨酸	异亮氨酸	亮氨酸	缬氨酸	丝氨酸	谷氨酸

（3）真核生物的细胞分裂从间期进入前期，除了核膜、核仁消失外，在显微镜下还可观察到________和________的出现。

46.（13分）豌豆子叶黄色（Y）与绿色（y）为一对等位基因控制，现将子叶黄色豌豆与子叶绿色豌豆杂交，F_1 自花授粉后结出 F_2 代种子共8 003粒，其中子叶黄色豌豆种子为6 002粒。试分析回答：

（1）________为显性性状，________为隐性性状。

（2）亲本的基因型为________和________。

（3）F_1 代产生配子的类型是________，其比例是__________。

（4）F_2 的表现型是________和________，其比例是__________，其中子叶绿色为________粒。

（5）F_2 的基因型是__________，其比例是____________。

（6）上述遗传现象属于基因的______________________规律。

47.（14分）下图为某草原生态系统（ecosystem）食物网（food web）图，请据图回答下列问题：

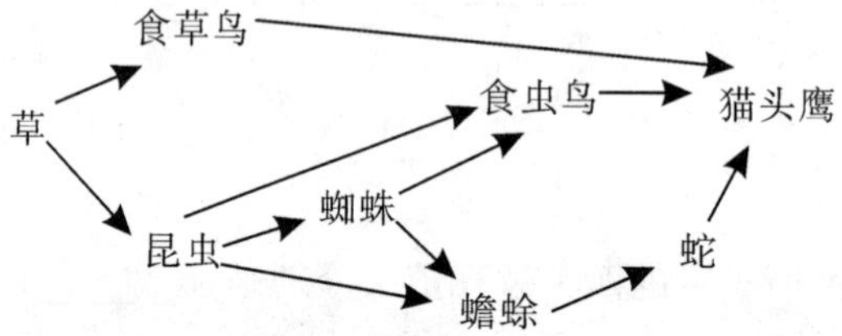

（1）这个食物网中有________条食物链，属于生产者（producer）的是________，可属于初级消费者（primary consumer）的是________，可属于次级消费者（secondary consumer）的有____________。

（2）图中的草属于第______营养级，昆虫属于第______营养级，属于第四营养级的生物有______，猫头鹰占有______个营养级，分别是第______营养级。

（3）蜘蛛和蟾蜍之间的种间关系，既是______关系，又是______关系。

暨南大学、华侨大学联合招收港澳地区、台湾省、华侨、华人及其他外籍学生入学考试样题

生　物

答题卡

一、选择题（共60分）

1 [A] [B] [C] [D]　6 [A] [B] [C] [D]　11 [A] [B] [C] [D]　16 [A] [B] [C] [D]
2 [A] [B] [C] [D]　7 [A] [B] [C] [D]　12 [A] [B] [C] [D]　17 [A] [B] [C] [D]
3 [A] [B] [C] [D]　8 [A] [B] [C] [D]　13 [A] [B] [C] [D]　18 [A] [B] [C] [D]
4 [A] [B] [C] [D]　9 [A] [B] [C] [D]　14 [A] [B] [C] [D]　19 [A] [B] [C] [D]
5 [A] [B] [C] [D]　10 [A] [B] [C] [D]　15 [A] [B] [C] [D]　20 [A] [B] [C] [D]

21 [A] [B] [C] [D]　26 [A] [B] [C] [D]
22 [A] [B] [C] [D]　27 [A] [B] [C] [D]
23 [A] [B] [C] [D]　28 [A] [B] [C] [D]
24 [A] [B] [C] [D]　29 [A] [B] [C] [D]
25 [A] [B] [C] [D]　30 [A] [B] [C] [D]

二、判断题（共20分）

31 [T] [F]　36 [T] [F]
32 [T] [F]　37 [T] [F]
33 [T] [F]　38 [T] [F]
34 [T] [F]　39 [T] [F]
35 [T] [F]　40 [T] [F]

以下为非选择题答题区，必须用黑色字迹的钢笔或签字笔在指定的黑色框区域内作答，否则答案无效。

三、简答题（共70分）

41.（6分，每个空格1分）

(1) ______________ ______________
(2) ______________ ______________
(3) ______________ ______________

42.（9分，每个空格1分）

①—______　②—______　③—______　④—______　⑤—______
⑥—______　⑦—______　⑧—______　⑨—______

43.（12 分，每个空格 1 分）

（1）______ ______ ______

（2）______ ______ ______ ______

（3）______ ______ ______

（4）______ ______

44.（10 分，每个空格 1 分）

（1）______、______、______、______

（2）______ （3）______

（4）______

（5）______ ______

（6）______

45.（6 分）

（1）______ ______（2 分）

（2）______（2 分）

（3）______ ______（2 分）

46.（13 分，每个空格 1 分）

（1）______ ______

（2）______ ______

（3）______ ______

（4）______ ______ ______ ______

（5）______ ______

（6）______

47.（14 分）

（1）______ ______ ______ ______（5 分）

（2）______ ______ ______ ______ ______（7 分）

（3）______ ______（2 分）

生物参考答案

一、选择题（本大题共30小题，每小题2分，共60分。每小题给出的四个选项中，只有一个选项最符合题目要求。请将正确答案按题号填涂在答题卡上）

1. A　2. C　3. C　4. C　5. D　6. B　7. B　8. C　9. C　10. B

11. C　12. D　13. D　14. D　15. C　16. C　17. C　18. D　19. C　20. C

21. A　22. A　23. B　24. A　25. D　26. D　27. D　28. C　39. D　30. B

二、判断题（对的画"T"，错的画"F"。本大题共10小题，每小题2分，共20分。请将正确答案按题号填涂在答题卡上）

31. T　32. F　33. F　34. F　35. F　36. F　37. F　38. T　39. T　40. T

三、简答题（共70分）

41.（6分，每个空格1分）

（1）淀粉　I　（2）还原糖　II　（3）加快　加快

42.（9分，每个空格1分）

①—E，②—A，③—F，④—B，⑤—G，⑥—C，⑦—H，⑧—D，⑨—I

43.（12分，每个空格1分）

（1）减数第一次　前（或减数前1）　8

（2）减数第一次　后（或减数后1）　初级精母细胞　次级精母细胞

（3）减数第二次分裂后　次级卵母细胞　卵细胞和极体

（4）1∶1　2∶1

44.（10分，每个空格1分）

（1）DNA复制　转录　翻译　逆转录

（2）c

（3）a

（4）细胞核

（5）tRNA（转运RNA）　氨基酸

（6）abc

45.（6分）

（1）解旋酶　半保留（2分）

（2）酪氨酸—谷氨酸—亮氨酸—谷氨酸—酪氨酸（2分）

（3）染色体　纺锤体（2分）

46.（13分，每个空格1分）

（1）子叶黄色　子叶绿色

（2）YY　yy

(3) Y 和 y　1∶1

(4) 子叶黄色　子叶绿色　3∶1　2 001

(5) YY，Yy，yy　1∶2∶1

(6) 基因分离

47. (14 分)

(1) 5　草　食草鸟、昆虫　食虫鸟、蜘蛛、蟾蜍、猫头鹰 (5 分)

(2) 一　二　蟾蜍、蛇、食虫鸟、猫头鹰　4　三、四、五、六 (7 分)

(3) 竞争　捕食 (2 分)

后　记

《暨南大学、华侨大学联合招收港澳地区、台湾省、华侨、华人及其他外籍学生入学考试复习大纲（2012—2015）》2015 年到期。为了更好地做好考纲修订工作，暨南大学、华侨大学两校组团到港澳部分中学进行了调研。调研结束后，两校联招办委托暨南大学华文学院预科部承担《暨南大学、华侨大学联合招收港澳地区、台湾省、华侨、华人及其他外籍学生入学考试复习大纲（2016—2020）》的修订工作。暨南大学华文学院的领导非常重视这项工作，并给予了大力的支持。为了做好这项工作，预科部从事预科教学的专家、学者，本着认真、严谨、科学的精神，考虑到内地和港澳台教育、教学的实际情况，结合对调研小组收集到的各种意见进行了多次的讨论分析，最后拿出了修订后的新考纲。

我们相信，新考纲对港澳地区、台湾省、华侨、华人和其他外籍学生报考暨南大学和华侨大学，将会起到很大的帮助作用。

预科部参与这次考纲修订的，主要有以下人员：

温宗军、岑文、张训涛、林娟、袁忠群、顾红、黄显麟、刘岑枫、刘家有、张卓、谢益民、赖章荣、谭学功、邓世军、陈芳、杨慧、覃儒奎、唐景阳、崔英超、黄小黎、蔡贤榜、李莹、姚蓓、李志红、谢晓华、何红卫。

其中各个科目的负责人为：

温宗军（中国语文）、赖章荣（数学）、陈芳（英语）、唐景阳（历史）、黄小黎（地理）、李莹（物理）、谢晓华（化学）、何红卫（生物）。

预科部主任温宗军副教授负责考纲修订工作的统筹安排，并负责对考纲内容进行统稿。

本书所有稿件最后由庄友明主编审定。

暨南大学、华侨大学联合招生委员会办公室
2015 年 3 月